Forms of ethical thinking in therapeutic practice

Forms of ethical thinking in therapeutic practice

Editors:
Derek Hill and Caroline Jones

Open University Press

Open University Press
McGraw-Hill Education
McGraw-Hill House
Shoppenhangers Road
Maidenhead
Berkshire
England
SL6 2QL

email: enquiries@openup.co.uk
world wide web: www.openup.co.uk

First published 2003

A catalogue record of this book is available from the British Library

ISBN 0 335 21278 6 (pb) 0 335 21279 4 (hb)

Library of Congress Cataloging-in-Publication Data
CIP data has been applied for

Typeset by RefineCatch Limited, Bungay, Suffolk
Printed and bound in Great Britain by MPG Books Ltd, Bodmin, Cornwall

To Jill and to Tony

Contents

Contributors

Kate Anthony runs OnlineCounsellors.co.uk, providing online and offline training for practitioners using the Internet, consultancy, media appearances, and international presentations on the topic. She is also a psychotherapist for a London Health Trust. Previous publications include co-authorship of the BACP *Guidelines for Online Counselling and Psychotherapy* and many journal articles.

Dr Mark Aveline MD, FRCPsych., Honorary Fellow of BACP, is Emeritus Consultant, Nottinghamshire Healthcare NHS Trust and President-elect, Society for Psychotherapy Research. In 2002 he retired after 27 years as consultant psychotherapist in Nottingham where he founded a 'one-stop' integrated specialist practice in psychodynamic and cognitive-behavioural psychotherapy. For several years he was in charge of specialist psychotherapy training in the Royal College of Psychiatrists, served on the governing board of the UKCP and was President of the BACP.

John Burnham has held a clinical and training practice at Regional CAMHS (Birmingham) since 1977. He was appointed as Consultant Family Therapist 1990 and has been Director of Training at Kensington Consultation Centre since 1990. Author of *Family Therapy* (Tavistock, 1986), he has also written over 20 journal papers and contributions to edited collections. John teaches, supervises and consults widely in the UK and abroad.

Suzanne Cerfontyne is a systemic psychotherapist who has worked with Birmingham CAMHS for 17 years. She provides clinical and training practice at Tiers 3 and 4. She is a trainer/supervisor on the Diploma in Systemic Therapy training course (University of Birmingham) at Parkview Clinic and has a private practice in clinical work and teaching/supervision.

Dr Stephen Goss is the Research Development Manager with the

British Association for Counselling and Psychotherapy (BACP) and Hon. Research Fellow with the University of Strathclyde and a qualified counsellor and supervisor. He was the lead author of the *BACP Guidelines for Online Counselling and Psychotherapy* (2001) and has produced numerous other works relating to innovative counselling practices, service evaluation and evidence-based practices.

Joan Guénault has been a Samaritan volunteer for 30 years, responding to callers by telephone, face-to-face and email. Initially her 'day job' was lecturing in higher education. She concurrently served 11 years on the Samaritans' governing body: as Branch Director, Regional Representative and finally Vice-Chair. She was then appointed to the central staff as Director of Training, serving in that post for nine years.

Derek Hill retired from the post of Head of Practitioner Training at Relate in 2000 after more than 25 years of couple casework, and engagements in supervision and training. A Fellow of BACP, he now combines writing with the demands of the role of Chair of the International Commission on Couple and Family Relations (ICCFR/CIRCF).

Caroline Jones is a workplace counsellor with 18 years' experience in this setting. She also has an independent practice as a counselling supervisor. She is one of the authors of *Questions of Ethics in Counselling and Therapy* (Open University Press, 2000). She is a senior registered counsellor and Fellow of BACP.

Dr Lina Kashyap is a Professor and Head of Department of Family and Child Welfare at the Tata Institute of Social Sciences, Mumbai (Bombay). She teaches courses related to social work practice with children, families and persons with a disability and is actively involved with voluntary welfare organizations in this field. She is currently the Vice-President of the International Association for Counselling and has published many articles and research papers in India and abroad.

Carol Shillito-Clarke is a Chartered Counselling Psychologist, a BACP Fellow and a BACP senior registered counsellor and supervisor. Over the past 25 years she has trained and worked as an integrative therapist, supervisor, trainer, lecturer and consultant in both the private and public sectors. She has a private practice in Warwick.

Sheelagh Strawbridge is a freelance Chartered Counselling Psychologist. She has experience in university teaching and professional training and is involved in committee work for the British Psychological Society. Her publications include *Exploring Self and Society* (with Rosamund Billington and Jenny Hockey; Macmillan, 1998) and she is an editor of *The Handbook of Counselling Psychology* (2nd edn, Sage, 2003).

Joan Wynn is a systemic psychotherapist working at regional CAMHS in Birmingham since 1998. She is a trainer and supervisor on the Post-Graduate Training in Systemic Family Therapy course and course coordinator and trainer on the Introductory Course in Systemic Family Therapy at Parkview Clinic, Birmingham. She has an independent systemic clinical practice including psychosexual therapy.

Foreword

Alan Jamieson *

The past two decades have seen significant developments in ethical thinking. It is important that such developments should in turn be reflected in and integrated into best professional practice. This is as true of the profession of counselling and psychotherapy as any other. Such changes, when they occur in professions, tend to be evolutionary and in many respects this strikes me as a good thing since it allows for changes in thinking to be assimilated into practice in a manner that benefits both service users, be they called clients or patients, and the practitioners involved.

There has also been a shift away from ethical bases that were generally held to be value-free to a position in which intrinsic values are acknowledged as underlying all statements of ethics and need to be made explicit. The debate between those who hold that we live in a world in which there are no moral values, and those who hold that there are, has exercised moral philosophers for many a year. It has been a long, complex and difficult one but, suffice to say, it has informed and been reflected in the thinking of the professions. That thinking has in its turn informed and influenced the professions in their view of what constitutes ethics and ethical practice. In the UK, in particular, we have, since at least the mid-1970s, seen a shift away from rule-based approaches to ethics to models based more on principles of accountability and awareness of the frames of values within society.

In addition to this, developments in therapeutic practice have also been very much informed by the growing corpus of experience and evidence within the professions connected with the interpersonal therapies. Add to this the impact of other societal changes that are in turn manifested in the counselling room, such as feminism,

* Alan Jamieson has recently been involved in the development and introduction of the *Ethical Framework for Good Practice in Counselling and Psychotherapy*, © BACP 2002.

human rights, bioethics and genetics to mention but a few, and it can be seen what very complex sets of constructs and situations counsellors and psychotherapists are required to work with.

Of real importance to practitioners seeking to work in an ethical manner is the provision of practice-informed guidance. This offers the opportunity to bring the products of thought and experience built up over many years to bear on the practice of those involved in counselling and therapy. This book is a valuable addition to the slowly growing canon of published guidance on ethics in practice. The range of contexts and activities covered helps us to see how modern ethical theory translates into practice in work with clients and patients. That the book takes a lateral approach with no attachment to any single model or way of working is to its credit, as are the facts that it includes a wide range of practice settings and that it embraces modern technologies which themselves can present new sets of ethical challenges. As such it will help practitioners realize a state of ethical mindfulness in their practice which in turn will require of them an enhanced awareness of individual values and moral qualities. Hopefully, it will also assist in the development of understanding of the way in which values have the potential both to inform and to impede professional ethical practice.

Alan Jamieson
Fellow of BACP

Introduction

There are a number of books available on ethics in therapy, such as Holmes and Lindley (1998), Tjeltveit (1999), Bond (2000) and Palmer Barnes and Murdin (2001), so the question 'Why another?' is a reasonable one. This book approaches ethical thinking in practice in a different way. The focus is an examination, within one book, of the differences and similarities of approaches to ethical thinking in therapy in the range of modalities and media, based on practice mainly in the UK and, in one chapter, India. It will be of interest to practitioners who want to know more about other therapeutic modalities and media and the ethical thinking that underpins these. It is of interest to practitioners who want to expand their ways of thinking about ethical practice, to inform their practice with clients, and who want to explore new perspectives.

A paradox is faced whenever efforts are made to generalize about the application of ethics to therapeutic practice since each and every dilemma has unique features. Dilemmas, where the application of ethical principles to a particular situation may require the choosing of one principle above another, are faced in each form of therapeutic practice and the choices made to resolve these are influenced by a number of factors. These include the nature of the theoretical approach, the personal philosophy, values and qualities of the therapist, and the setting, cultural and the social contexts. While many practitioners develop an awareness of the ethical requirements of their own form(s) of practice, we believe that practice can be enriched by a comparative study of the ethical approaches of our own and other therapeutic forms and by developing an active awareness of our own social and cultural context. In the absence of such knowledge, and in the context of multidisciplinary teams, and the movements of clients from one form of therapeutic resource to another, misunderstandings and confusion can result about the differences in handling ethical issues. More seriously, poor and unethical practice can result in harm to clients and complaints against the practitioner, as described by Palmer Barnes (1998) and Casemore (2001). In the UK, POPAN

(Prevention of Professional Abuse Network) performs a valuable service to clients who have been harmed by therapy or by their therapist.

This book describes a number of different approaches and kinds of thinking used to address ethical dilemmas that arise within the various forms of and contexts of psychotherapeutic practice and complements existing texts on ethics practised within specific modalities and media. The book outlines the influences that result in the adoption of different approaches to ethical issues in the various forms of therapy. It demonstrates how those influences arise from the nature of the therapeutic transactions that characterize each form, from the differing social contexts in which therapy is undertaken and as a consequence of the therapeutic medium being used.

There is no single preferred approach to ethical thinking and it is rarely possible to identify a sole 'correct' way to resolve a specific dilemma. Therefore, it remains a practitioner's responsibility to be rigorous in their thinking and to take all pertinent factors into account. Many therapists will make use of their supervision to talk through the dilemmas that arise in their work with clients. Where a dilemma is particularly urgent, those with regular supervisory arrangements (see Chapter 9) will also be able to contact their supervisor between booked sessions. Therapists who are members of the British Association for Counselling and Psychotherapy (BACP) and the United Kingdom Association for Humanistic Psychology Practitioners (UKAHPP) have an additional and valuable source of help. The BACP offers an ethical helpline to members. When queries are especially challenging, a network of experienced practitioners are 'on call' to assist. This resource helps the practitioner with their thinking towards resolving the dilemma they face (see Chapter 10). The UKAHPP has a more formal ethical review procedure that enables 'clarification as to whether a proposed course of action would constitute an ethical violation' (UKAHPP 2003) and is open to its members and their clients. This procedure, over time, informs revisions to that association's ethical principles and codes of practice.

The timing of seeking and entering counselling or therapy is often significant and the timing of undertaking this book also has its own significance. This is a follow-on volume to *Questions of Ethics in Counselling and Therapy* (Jones *et al.* 2000), where the focus was on ethics and dilemmas in the practice of individual and couple counselling and therapy. While *Questions of Ethics* was being written in 1998–2000, the BACP was in the process of producing a radically new approach to ethical practice. This approach challenges its member practitioners in new ways and aims to offer a relevant ethical framework to the widest range of therapeutic modalities and media, in any setting and irrespective of therapeutic approach. The *Ethical Framework for Good Practice in Counselling and Psychotherapy* (BACP 2002) is now in use. A document so innovative merits attention and we acknowledge it as a catalyst for this book. The contributors also draw upon the codes of their own and other professional associations. There are a number of professional codes and statements of ethics in the world of therapy, each with its own emphases and priorities.

The book opens with a chapter that discusses the place of ethical thinking in therapeutic practice. Ethical mindfulness requires more from a therapist than adherence to codes of practice, and Sheelagh Strawbridge sets the scene by exploring the complexities of ethical thinking. She looks at a number of themes, including issues of professional expertise and the tensions between the 'doing-to' and 'being-with' in therapy.

Chapters 2–8 examine the ways that ethical issues are addressed in specific therapeutic modalities and media. Caroline Jones draws on her experience as a workplace counsellor to examine the ethical thinking that underpins individual therapy in Chapter 2, with its focus on autonomy and fidelity. In Chapter 3, Joan Guénault writes about telephone work, based upon her experience with the Samaritans, and this chapter provides a fascinating insight to this important area of work with callers, of whom there were in excess of 4 million in 2001. The Samaritans' mission statement is provided as an appendix to this book.

'Ethical thinking in online therapy' (Chapter 4), describes the new challenges presented by this approach to offering therapy, and Kate Anthony and Stephen Goss outline a number of existing ethical challenges, such as confidentiality, in a modality that is under pressure from evolving technology. In Chapter 5, Derek Hill draws upon his extensive experience with Relate to describe ethical thinking in couple work with its challenge to engage partners in the work on the relationship.

In Chapter 6, Dr Lina Kashyap describes the ethical issues in family and marital counselling and how these are addressed in the complex culture of India. She describes a society where marriage is perceived as a socio-religious institution while opportunities for women are opening up, resulting in changing expectations and creating ripples in family life. She has also provided (see Appendix 3) the Bombay Association of Trained Social Workers' Declaration of Ethics for Professional Social Workers which includes a value framework and pledge.

A group of family therapists, John Burnham, Suzanne Cerfontyne and Joan Wynn, have contributed the chapter on ethical thinking in family therapy (Chapter 7), exploring, for example, the complexities of confidentiality within the room. In Chapter 8, Dr Mark Aveline draws on his extensive experience on ethical thinking relating to group work where, for example, the needs of the individual sometimes have to be weighed against the needs of the group.

Chapters 2–8 have been organized in a consistent way to make it easy to see their common ground and to draw comparisons between the different ways of working. These chapters contain three elements: characteristics of the modality/medium; critical situations and their ethical resolution; and suggestions relating to emergent issues in ethical practice. Using the same chapter structure, in Chapter 9, Carol Shillito-Clarke considers the ethical thinking and challenges of supervision, since for many practitioners this is a mandatory and essential element of ethical practice. In the final chapter, we, the editors, have taken the opportunity to draw together themes and make comparisons and links between the content presented. Our purposes are to facilitate ethical thinking within the reader's form(s) of practice, to clarify the ethical demands of different forms of therapy, and to discuss the challenges that lie ahead.

Readers may wish to read Chapters 2–9 in an order different from that in which they are presented, perhaps choosing to look at the unfamiliar modalities and media first. Each of these chapters is self-contained. We invite you to reflect on the ways in which the contributors meet the challenges of their particular client groups and settings, and we recommend reading all other chapters before Chapter 10. An author index is included for authors referenced as source material, but not those listed as background. Useful addresses, including all the professional associations whose codes and other material have been referred to, are provided in an appendix.

Finally, we wish to thank all the contributors for their collaboration in this endeavour. We and our contributors are grateful for the support and encouragement of family members and colleagues.

Derek Hill
Caroline Jones

References

BACP (2002) *Ethical Framework for Good Practice in Counselling and Psychotherapy*. Rugby: British Association for Counselling and Psychotherapy.

Bond, T. (2000) *Standards and Ethics in Counselling*, 2nd edn. London: Sage.

Casemore, R. (2001) *Surviving Complaints against Counsellors and Psychotherapists: Towards Understanding and Healing*. Ross-on-Wye: PCCS Books.

Holmes, J. and Lindley, R. (1998) *The Values of Psychotherapy* (rev. edn). London: Karnac.

Jones, C., Shillito-Clarke, C., Syme, G. *et al.* (2000) *Questions of Ethics in Counselling and Therapy*. Buckingham: Open University Press.

Palmer Barnes, F. (1998) *Complaints and Grievances in Psychotherapy: A Handbook of Ethical Practice*. London: Routledge.

Palmer Barnes, F. and Murdin, L. (2001) *Values and Ethics in the Practice of Psychotherapy and Counselling*. Buckingham: Open University Press.

Tjeltveit, A.C. (1999) *Ethics and Values in Psychotherapy*. London: Routledge.

UKAHPP (2003) Ethical review procedure, in *Handbook and National Membership Register*. London: United Kingdom Association for Humanistic Psychology Practitioners.

Abbreviations

ACA	American Counseling Association
AFT	Association for Family Therapy
BACP	British Association for Counselling and Psychotherapy
BAP	British Association of Psychotherapists
BASRT	British Association for Sexual and Relationship Therapy
BCP	British Confederation of Psychotherapists
BPS	British Psychological Society
BPS, DCoP	British Psychological Society, Division of Counselling Psychology
CAMHS	Child and Adolescent Mental Health Services
CIRCF	Commission Internationale des Relations du Couple et de la Famille
CLI	Caller Line Identification
COSCA	Confederation of Scottish Counselling Agencies
CPD	continuing professional development
EAP	employee assistance programme
FCC	family counselling centres
IAC	International Association for Counselling
ICCFR	International Commission on Couple and Family Relations
IPN	Independent Practitioners Network
IRC	Internet relay chat
ISMHO	International Society for Mental Health Online
NBCC	National Board for Certified Counsellors
NMGC	National Marriage Guidance Council
NHS	National Health Service
POPAN	Prevention of Professional Abuse Network
TC	therapeutic community
THA	Telephone Helplines Association
TISS	Tata Institute of Social Science
UKAHPP	United Kingdom Association of Humanistic Psychology Practitioners
UKCP	United Kingdom Council for Psychotherapy
VO	voluntary organizations

1 Ethics, psychology and therapeutic practice[1]

Sheelagh Strawbridge

This chapter explores the place of ethical thinking in therapeutic practice. My perspective is shaped by a history of teaching social science and psychology before training in therapy, which I began with Relate. I have long been involved in the development of Counselling Psychology within the British Psychological Society. So my contribution is focused by an interest in the relationship between psychology and ethics. These disciplines can be seen as two central pillars supporting the professionalization of therapy and the interesting stage that this process has reached in the UK contextualizes the discussion. I argue that how the relationship between psychology and ethics is constructed has important implications for the way therapy is defined and the way it is practised. The chapter draws on social science and thus offers a somewhat different view from texts that attend more specifically to professional ethics and codes of practice, such as Bond (2000) and Jones *et al.* (2000), and from those that explore a broader ethical territory, such as Holmes and Lindley (1998) and Tjeltveit (1999).

Professionalization and regulation

The concern with ethical issues has grown in the context of professionalization. As Tjeltveit (1999: 255) notes: 'When psychotherapists assert that they are professionals, they announce, they profess, they make public testimony that they possess specialized knowledge and technical skills that help people with psychological problems.' A promise is made that the profession can be trusted to act in other than its own interests, so an ideology of public service and altruism is espoused. Hence the assertion of professional status implies both competence, in specialized knowledge and skills, and ethical commitment.

Of course, these claims are made by the emerging profession on its own behalf and in conjunction with the formation of a professional body representing its interests. So, against the ideal of altruism we must set the recognition that, since their origins, initially as law, medicine and the clergy, in the medieval universities, professions have been characterized by the monopolization of particular forms of expertise and the erection of social boundaries around themselves (Abbott and Wallace 1990: 2). They control entry through lengthy training and qualifications and are thus as much about exclusion and power as about service. Professional power has long been the subject of critiques from both left and right political perspectives and the demand for regulation can be seen both as a negative manifestation of power (for example Mowbray 1995) and as a genuine acknowledgement of, and desire to redress, abuses of power. Ethical frameworks, codes of practice and disciplinary procedures are, in part, aspects of self-regulation that serve to establish trust, by ensuring some protection for clients. They can thus be situated alongside legal and political frameworks, and ethical, legal and political issues inevitably interrelate.

Professionalization in the UK, as elsewhere, has had a complex history, marked by dissent, and resulting here in the formation of not one but four main professional bodies. Although evolving from earlier organizations, three have been established within the past 30 years: the British Association for Counselling (1977) and Psychotherapy (2000); the United Kingdom Standing Conference (1989)/ Council (1992) for Psychotherapy; and, the British Confederation of Psychotherapists (1992). The British Psychological Society has a longer history, being established in 1901 and incorporated by Royal Charter in 1965. However, it did not register chartered psychologists until 1987 and counselling psychologists were not chartered until 1992. It is now beginning to register chartered psychologists specializing in psychotherapy. The BACP and the BPS are membership organizations, whereas the UKCP and the BCP are umbrella organizations. Practitioners of therapy may be called counsellors, psychotherapists, counselling or clinical psychologists. So, particularly in moving towards regulation, the question has arisen as to whether we are talking about one or a number of different professions or perhaps one or two different kinds of activity (counselling and psychotherapy) that differing professions (including psychology and psychiatry) all practise.

Each professional body commits practitioners to ethical standards and codes of practice. The main concerns, in the context of self-regulation, are to protect clients/patients from bad practice, and with the ethos and conditions within which therapy takes place. To this end there is significant agreement across the codes about basic principles and standards of conduct. Ethical issues are seen largely as relating to aspects of conduct, such as the management of boundaries and the non-exploitation of clients, and to dilemmas arising in situations where values conflict, for example those of client autonomy and client safety. These are important areas of ethical thinking in relation to practice and some of the issues are explored in other chapters of this book. However, such issues, relating to the standards and conditions of practice, may be seen as external to the actual process of therapy, which is often, though not always, conceived in psychological rather than ethical terms. This is reflected in the way that ethics is often approached on training courses, with codes of ethics and practice being introduced (and trainees required to commit to them) but not discussed in depth. Training focuses on what is seen as the theory and practice of the approach or approaches to therapy itself. The way that the codes have been written, as rules, has no doubt contributed to this marginalization of ethical thinking.

Nevertheless, in the context of professionalization, ethics has begun to feature more significantly in the curriculum, usually as the kinds of issue and dilemma noted above. Moreover, the BACP has recently developed a fundamentally changed ethical framework and the BPS is engaged in a similar task. These two major professional bodies are moving away from an approach to professional conduct based on sets of rules, towards one based on values and principles. This will require those of us whose practice they govern to think differently about ethics. It will take time to establish, but the change is quite profound. Ethical thinking and reasoned judgements based on values and principles will be expected and there will be less specific guidance in the form of rules. Moreover, at least within the BACP framework, which draws as much on virtue ethics as on duty ethics, practitioners will be expected to cultivate personal qualities, such as empathy, sincerity and respect, considered to be characteristic of good therapists, as a matter of *ethical responsibility* as well as in the context of *technical competence*. This emphasis on personal qualities and values reorients the approach to professional ethics in a way that makes ethical thinking central to the process of therapy. Ashcroft notes, in an article introducing the new framework, that it does so precisely by drawing attention to the personal and moral qualities of the practitioner and stressing the personal dimension and the quality of the relationship in therapy. He states unequivocally that, 'Counselling and psychotherapy are thoroughly ethical activities, in the deepest sense of the term "ethical". They are concerned with the process of discovering the good life' (Ashcroft 2001: 10). Thus, in his view, the new framework *defines* therapy as a fundamentally ethical activity.

Of course, there are differing aspects of, and ways of characterizing, ethics. Bohme (2001) distinguishes three:

- A branch of academic philosophy, an area of knowledge of a specific kind with its own methods and schools.
- Connected with the idea of philosophy as a mode of living or a way of life.
- Practical wisdom.

The second and third of these characterizations have to do with what Bohme calls 'the art of dealing with serious questions'. Ashcroft is clearly linking therapy with the second, where ethical or moral questions are seen as arising when matters become serious for each of us individually. Bohme argues that how we decide those questions determines who we are and how we regard ourselves. They are questions that have to do with 'being-human-well' or virtue ethics. The third characterization of ethics, as practical wisdom, centres on public as distinct from personal concerns. Here the basic values of communal life are at issue and arguments involve the formation of public opinion as a background for social regulation. So ethical or moral questions arise when matters become serious for a community and affect how it regards itself and what it becomes. In this aspect it is easy to see the interrelationship of ethics and politics.

Ethics and psychology

All this points to areas of contested, or at least shared, ground between ethics and psychology, of central relevance to therapy.

Engaging with clients about issues relating to who they are and how they regard themselves is clearly an ethical activity as defined above. Moreover, ethics as practical wisdom seems to be what we engage in when we publicly debate the nature of therapy, how we regard it and what it should become, particularly in relation to regulation. On the other hand, psychological theories, explicitly or implicitly, contain normative notions about the nature of persons, their well-being and potential, and debates between theoretical approaches and models of therapy can be seen as debates *within* psychology. Thus, questions about the relationship between ethics and psychology are fundamental in defining the profession. Whereas the new BACP framework stresses the ethical character of therapy and the centrality of personal qualities and relationship, the claim to expertise and the possession of specialized knowledge and technical skills is frequently made on the basis of psychology. So the relation between ethics and psychology involves a tension which can be usefully expressed in terms of Buber's (1958) distinction between two modes of being-in-relation, 'I–It' and 'I–Thou'. This can translate into seeing ourselves, as practitioners, as either technical experts or as persons in relation.

Interestingly, there is a wealth of psychological research evidence demonstrating the therapeutic significance of the practitioner–client relationship. Roth and Fonagy (1996) clearly confirm this, and Hubble *et al.* (1999), in their analysis of outcome research, identify client variables and extra-therapeutic factors as accounting for as much as 40 per cent of improvement in therapy and the therapeutic relationship as accounting for 30 per cent. Placebo/expectancy effects and specific techniques each account for 15 per cent. Moreover, the evidence that, in terms of overall effectiveness, no one therapeutic approach is better than any other is persuasive (Lambert and Bergin 1994). This seems to underscore the emphasis of the BACP framework. Nonetheless, despite the evidence, professionalization favours a stress on technical competence and an increasing reliance on therapeutic techniques. 'Doing-to' is emphasized over a relationship in which 'being-with' a person is paramount; 'I–It' takes precedence over 'I–Thou' irrespective of the therapeutic approach. Lomas (1999) has, for instance, drawn attention to the increasing emphasis on technique over relationship within the psychoanalytic tradition. He explores some of the ways in which what he terms 'the retreat from the ordinary' damages the therapeutic process and diverts attention from its personal and ethical dimensions.

Of course, this seeming 'ordinariness' of 'being-in-relation' is part of the problem. It can appear to undermine the claim to professional expertise. Nevertheless, Carl Rogers, who did much to establish the significance of relationship in therapeutic processes, stressed that therapeutic relationships are *not* different *in kind* from relationships in everyday life. What can be overlooked is the intrinsic value of meeting when depth of contact can be established in the relationship. Rogers emphasized the *extraordinary* therapeutic potential of this *ordinary* human capacity and we owe much to his careful work in researching its nature and potential and for identifying such key therapeutic factors as acceptance, empathy and congruence.

Differing therapeutic approaches now draw upon this understanding and one might expect it to lead to a more significant focus on research into the relationship and an exploration of issues that arise when this is considered in some depth. For example, while there are strong affinities between the approaches of Rogers and Buber, there are significant differences with implications for practice (Kirschenbaum and Henderson 1990: 41–63; Friedman 1992). It is possible, in the area of relationship, to imagine ethical and psychological inquiry as complementary. Indeed, deepening our understanding of acceptance, empathy and congruence requires this as they relate to psychological attributes and skills of the therapist, to her or his ethical virtues and to the declared values of therapeutic practice. Moreover, whatever the approach, in the specificity of each therapeutic relationship, questions arise which have both ethical and psychological aspects, such as: 'What does it mean to encounter this person?', 'What is my responsibility to this particular other?', 'How will I use my professional power in this specific relationship?', 'How will aspects of my self and my values enter this relationship through, for example, disclosing aspects of my personal experience?', 'When and how will I offer or withhold insights, interpretations or specific techniques?'

More commonly, the relationship is considered superficially and reduced to a precondition for the application of techniques, the 'technical expert' overshadows the 'person-in-relation'. This stress on technical expertise can be linked both to the employment context and to the way psychology has developed as a discipline, traditionally adopting a 'natural science' model. It is favoured by professional recognition and the increasing employment of therapists in organizations (significantly the NHS and employee assistance programmes) where a heavy demand on resources is coupled with a justifiable expectation of accountability.

Such settings tend to promote short-term problem- or solution-focused work and standardized, manualized and even computerized treatments to the exclusion of more flexible, creative approaches (which stress the specificity of each therapeutic relationship) and longer-term, in-depth work. There is a strong demand for evidence-based practice which encourages research conforming to the dominant 'natural science' model and a bias towards cognitive-behavioural therapy. This best fits the model and, importantly for a profession working increasingly in medically dominated contexts, can strengthen claims to a distinctive field of *psychologically defined* expertise validated by research (for example British Psychological Society, Division of Clinical Psychology 2000). However, much research can be criticized for being constrained by notions of good design inappropriate to complex life situations (Spinelli 2001: 5). The emphasis is on efficacy studies, characterized by 'randomized control trials', though, as Seligman (1995) argues, these may not be the best way to evaluate the effectiveness of therapy (and see Mace *et al.* 2001). Moreover, exaggerated claims can be made about the significance of results or the adequacy of the design (see, for example, debates initiated by Bolsover 2001 and Holmes 2002).

Psychology: a natural science?

Despite the weight of theory and research that challenges it, the 'natural science' view of modern psychology, although modified, is still mainstream and supported by a long history. Its development, in the second half of the nineteenth century, as psychology emerged as one of the disciplines aiming to study human beings scientifically, can be understood as part of a wider social and historical process, conceptualized as 'rationalization' by Weber (1974).

Rationalization involves the application of rational decision-making criteria to increasing areas of social life and is linked with the rise of industrial capitalism in the West. Progressively freed from the external constraint of values (historically the 'Protestant ethic'), productivity becomes an end in itself as opposed to a means whereby independently identified human needs can be satisfied. The effect is to construct a complex 'iron cage' of bureaucratic rules and regulations geared to calculable economic efficiency (Weber 1974: 180–2). Different spheres of life are increasingly separated and subject to specialization and the creation of technical experts, forming what Habermas (1971) terms 'subsystems of instrumental action'. Rationality is reduced to a single form, 'instrumental rationality', and defined entirely in terms of the most efficient means to achieve subsystem-specific goals, such as 'productivity', 'scientific truth' and 'technological progress'. Imagination, emotional experience, the arts and moral values are all effectively excluded from the sphere of reason and truth (Abbs 1996: 31–45). The model of professional practice that arises casts practitioners in the role of instrumental problem-solvers applying technical expertise to well-formed problems. Schön, in offering an alternative 'reflective practitioner' model, argues that it falsely suggests

> a high, hard ground overlooking a swamp. On the high ground, manageable problems lend themselves to solution through the application of research based theory and technique. [However] In the swampy lowland, messy, confusing problems defy technical solution. . . . [And] in the swamp lie the problems of greatest human concern.
>
> (Schön 1987: 3)

In tune with the process of rationalization, in which technological and social progress are linked, traditional 'scientific' psychology is rooted in the Enlightenment philosophies of empiricism and positivism. It stresses knowledge claims based on 'objectively observable facts' verifiable against 'sense-experience'. This emphasis on objectivity and observability favours the study of behaviour rather than subjective experience. Laws allowing the prediction and control of behaviour are sought which, once discovered, can be applied to the treatment of criminality and mental illness, the assessment of abilities and aptitudes, the education of children, the organization of the workplace, and so on. This merely indicates how psychology positioned itself historically as a natural science (see also Strawbridge and Woolfe 2003) but, as such, its continuing concern is the pursuit of objectivity and truth. While ethical questions are asked about the conduct of research and the application of its findings, they are seen as external to the discipline itself. Human beings are approached as objects of systematic study, not as subjects interacting with researchers and their findings. The model is inherently deterministic and generates causal explanations that locate control outside the agency of those controlled.

The psychological theories underpinning therapeutic practices are often broadly understood as scientific in this sense. This strengthens the emphasis on technical expertise, particularly in clinical settings with a biomedical ethos. Ethical considerations are focused on issues relating to applications and professional conduct, following traditional approaches to medical ethics. However, as Hacking argues, even psychiatric classifications with a possible biological basis, such as schizophrenia, are 'interactive', always open to revision because 'people classified in a certain way change in response to being classified' (Hacking 1999: 123). Moreover, the very range of competing psychological theories and therapeutic approaches suggests that theoretical concepts, relating to such things as the nature of persons, their well-being, potential and pathology, are value-laden. Adopting a natural science model of psychology, with its technical expertise model of practice, encourages avoidance of ethical and political debate about the values embedded in such differing therapeutic approaches. It militates against viewing therapy as a *fundamentally* ethical activity.

The human science alternative

The natural science model of psychology has, however, been contested from the start. As psychology, history, sociology, economics and social anthropology emerged as empirical disciplines, claims were made that their subject matter is crucially different from that of the natural sciences and requires differing methods of study. In Britain, John Stuart Mill coined the term 'moral sciences' to distinguish these disciplines. They were termed *Geisteswissenschaften* in German, which can translate as 'human sciences'. The German philosopher William Dilthey linked the notion of human science to a theory of understanding and he significantly influenced the development of research into human consciousness, subjective experience, meaning and culture. Consciousness and human agency are emphasized in the human science model, and values are inseparable from its assumption that human beings have the capacity for choice and personal responsibility, as opposed to being entirely determined by internal and external causes. Methods appropriate to the study of self-conscious, reflective and self-determining beings are sought.

Nonetheless, in Britain and America, the natural science model predominated throughout the social sciences and psychology, at least until the 1960s. By that time, in a general climate of humanism generated by political and intellectual upheaval, human science approaches were gaining ground. Humanistic psychology, associated with Carl Rogers and Abraham Maslow and rooted in the European phenomenological tradition, was among them. Its emphasis on freewill and human potential was significant in the political context and counselling first evolved as one of a range of democratizing practices in humanistic psychology (Herman 1992). The quality of the therapeutic relationship was stressed together with the validity of the subjective experience and capacity for self-determination and personal responsibility of the person in the client role.

Humanistic psychology, with its stress on values and relationships, remains an important influence. However, while championing human subjectivity and freewill, it courts utopian ideas of democracy and human perfectibility. Rogers, for example, was challenged, from a more existential viewpoint, by May for neglecting the human capacity for evil (Kirschenbaum and Henderson 1990: 239–51), and Spinelli (1989: 159) contends that humanistic psychology adopts an overoptimistic view of human nature and human freedom. Additionally, the emphasis on 'self-actualization' can lead to a neglect of the self-in-relation, and questions of responsibility to others.

The more general humanism of the early 1960s similarly overemphasized the responsibility of individuals for their own circumstances and life-chances. 'Structuralist' critiques drew upon structuralist linguistics, which defines languages as structured symbolic systems. From this perspective, subjective consciousness, structured by language, could be viewed as socially constructed and more obviously available for scientific study. Human action was understood as generated within symbolic meaning systems in which socio-political power is legitimated in ideologies. Marxist and feminist studies were particularly important in showing how these power relations are reproduced through the construction of personal identities (see, for example, Billington *et al.* 1998: 52–7). As the structures of language and ideology operate, as it were, beneath consciousness, social science renewed its interest in psychoanalytic studies, particularly through the work of Jacques Lacan, who, influenced by structuralist linguistics, claimed, 'the unconscious is structured like a language' (1977: 20).

'Structuralism', again overdeterministic, in turn became a focus of critique, and 'post-structuralism' linked with a broader set of complex and debatable ideas – 'postmodernism' – emerged. It maintains a similar view of the relation between language and consciousness to structuralism, but rejects the conception of languages as large, unified systems in favour of smaller systems or 'discourses' located in specific forms of social life. Like Weber, post-structuralists and postmodernists argue that life is inherently multifarious and contradictory and all thinking and evaluation limited within perspectives. They contend that grand theories and overarching systems of thought, 'meta-narratives', are oppressive and, in recognizing the varied forms of social life, its 'little narratives', postmodernism has a liberating potential (Lyotard 1984). Postmodernism and post-structuralism have influenced a range of approaches to the study of human beings that have gained significance in psychology. These approaches include social constructionism, discourse analysis, conversation analysis, deconstruction and critical psychology. Alongside developments in phenomenological research and psychoanalysis, these approaches have contributed much to the study of subjective experience, social relationships and personal identity by rigorous qualitative methods (see, for example, Smith *et al.* 1995).

Ethics, psychology and practice, challenge and change

Language thus provides a crucial key, unlocking possibilities for studying conscious and unconscious meanings and motivations, culture and ideology. Moreover, the relationship between structure and agency can be explored as a function of how subjective consciousness, while structured by discourses, has the capacity for self-reflection and choice. All this has strengthened the human science model and re-established the significance of critique and the centrality of ethical and political values. If knowledge is always limited within perspectives, then those perspectives must be made transparent and their implicit values examined. Studies within psychology, which are beginning the self-reflective critique of the discipline (for example Burman 1994; Fox and Prilleltensky 1997), demonstrate that, far from being value-free, psychology plays a key role in constructing and maintaining socio-political structures and power relationships. Michel Foucault's work has been particularly useful in showing how. Psychological theories, viewed as discourses, can be seen to operate within a 'general politics' or 'regime of truth': that is, 'the types of discourse which [a society] accepts and makes function as true'. Consistent with the process of rationalization, in societies like ours 'truth' 'is centred on the form of scientific discourse and the institutions which produce it' (Gordon 1980: 131).

More specifically, studies of the discourses of psychopathology and psychotherapy pose a considerable ethical and political challenge to established therapeutic practice (for example Parker *et al.* 1995; Parker 1999; Fee 2000; Hook and Eagle 2002). They show how, whatever the model, biomedical/psychiatric, cognitive-behavioural, psychoanalytic or humanistic, theories situate clients and their problems within normative discourses that, for example, set standards of mental health, adjustment, development or self-realization. Moreover, they position the therapist as expert and privilege the language of the model over the everyday language of clients. In doing so they often oppress the people they intend to help. Writing from a post-Jungian perspective, Hillman (1983: 15) has noted the power of such psychological stories:

> Once one has been written into a particular clinical fantasy with its expectations, its typicalities, its character traits, and the rich vocabulary it offers for recognizing oneself, one then begins to recapitulate one's life into the shape of the story. One's past too is retold and finds a new internal coherence, even inevitability, through this abnormal story.

So it seems that, in Bohme's terms, things are certainly becoming serious for the communal life of therapists. Ethics as 'practical wisdom' is very much on the agenda, particularly in the process of professionalization and regulation. Interestingly, this same process that emphasizes 'technical expertise', has also brought therapists of different persuasions into more contact through professional bodies. A good deal of conflict has ensued but, over time, it is possible to discern an increasing tolerance, and even respect, for difference. As noted above, the quality of the therapeutic relationship is stressed as the most significant common factor in effective therapy. So the standpoint of 'being-in-relation' is gaining support and is underlined by the new BACP ethical framework.

It seems that I have arrived back at the tension between 'doing-to' and 'being-with'. I struggle with the questions: 'How can I "be-in-relation" with my clients in a non-oppressive way which, nevertheless, does justice to my knowledge and understanding?' and 'What justification might there be for my claim to psychological understanding, and therapeutic expertise?' (Strawbridge 1999). Polkinghorne (1992) suggests a way forward. He argues that the limited relevance of academic psychology to practitioners has resulted in a psychology of practice with its own 'fragmented collection of discordant theories and techniques' based on actual interactions between practitioners and clients. Underlying the generation of knowledge through practice is an implicit 'postmodern epistemology'. It assumes that: there is no firm foundation for establishing indubitable truth; knowledge consists of fragments of understanding, 'little narratives', rather than large logically integrated systems; these fragments are constructed in cultures; and, knowledge is tested pragmatically, by its usefulness. This sits easily alongside Schön's 'reflective practitioner' model, and Polkinghorne, like Schön, links his 'postmodern epistemology of practice' to a range of studies of the ways in which professionals in a variety of disciplines actually develop and apply knowledge in practice.

Within this framework, when I am with an individual 'for whom matters have become serious,' I can, as therapist, draw upon the range of techniques and interpretive concepts available to me, in a spirit of cooperative inquiry. As we live our lives constructed in discourses, I can recognize that, while therapeutic discourses can oppress when imposed, they can also help to 'deconstruct' everyday discourses, which can be equally oppressive, and offer liberating alternatives. However, it is important not to claim too much for therapy and I believe there is an ethical imperative to interrogate and deconstruct our own theories and techniques, as we cannot ignore the socio-political contexts in which they are constructed. We must also strive to grasp the complexity of seeking to understand another person. According to Emmanuel Levinas, the very search for intelligibility that dominates western European philosophy implies reducing difference and otherness to the same. He proposes an alternative ethic of responsibility to the 'other' who is 'radically unknowable' (Davis 1996). There is a growing literature exploring the meaning and possibility of genuine dialogues between different voices and world-views (see, for example, Sampson 1993) and, in more concrete terms, postcolonial, black, feminist and gay literatures offer intimations of what it might be like to really appreciate difference, in the coexistence of alternative realities and multiple voices.

All this has profound implications for practice, which we are only beginning to explore. So we live in challenging and exciting times. An increasing awareness of the limited applicability of technical rational knowledge in therapy, despite the pressure to claim technical expertise, brings into focus value conflicts and the unavoidable responsibility we have to others. Many practice situations are vague and uncertain but decisions must be made and actions taken and accounted for. Social life is, in a real sense, radically open, and socio-political and moral concepts are 'essentially contestable' (Gallie 1956). Under these conditions, we must seek a new relationship between ethics and psychology so that they can together offer guiding principles and insightful conceptual frameworks that can inform our best efforts to 'be-in-relation' therapeutically with those 'others' who become our clients.

Note

1. Therapy and therapeutic are used as general terms to include counselling, psychotherapy and counselling/psychotherapeutic psychology.

References

Abbott, P. and Wallace, C. (eds) (1990) *The Sociology of the Helping Professions*. London: Falmer Press.

Abbs, P. (1996) *The Polemics of Imagination: Selected Essays on Art, Culture and Society*. London: Skoob Books.

Ashcroft, R. (2001) What's the good of counselling and psychotherapy: developing an ethical framework, *Counselling and Psychotherapy Journal*, 12(8): 10–12.

Billington, R., Hockey, J. and Strawbridge, S. (1998) *Exploring Self and Society*. London: Macmillan.

Bohme, G. (2001) *Ethics in Context: The Art of Dealing with Serious Questions*. Cambridge: Polity Press.

Bolsover, N. (2001) Correspondence with Peter Kinderman, *Clinical Psychology*, 5 and 6. Leicester: British Psychological Society.

Bond, T. (2000) *Standards and Ethics for Counselling in Action*, 2nd edn. London: Sage.

British Psychological Society, Division of Clinical Psychology (2000) *Recent Advances in Understanding Mental Illness and Psychotic Experiences*. Leicester: British Psychological Society.

Buber, M. (1958) *I and Thou*, trans. R.G. Smith. Edinburgh: T. & T. Clark.

Burman, E. (1994) *Deconstructing Developmental Psychology*. London: Routledge.

Davis, C. (1996) *Levinas: An Introduction*. Cambridge: Polity Press.

Fee, D. (ed.) (2000) *Pathology and the Postmodern: Mental Illness as Discourse and Experience*. London: Sage.

Fox, D. and Prilleltensky, I. (eds) (1997) *Critical Psychology: An Introduction*. London: Sage.

Friedman, M. (1992) *Dialogue and the Human Image: Beyond Humanistic Psychology*. London: Sage.

Gallie, W.B. (1956) Essentially contested concepts, *Proceedings of the Aristotelian Society*, 56: 167–98.

Gordon, C. (ed.) (1980) *Michel Foucault: Power / Knowledge – Selected Interviews and Other Writings, 1972–1977*. Brighton: Harvester.

Habermas, J. (1971) Technology and science as 'ideology', in *Toward a Rational Society*, trans. J.J. Shapiro. London: Heinemann.

Hacking, I. (1999) *The Social Construction of What?* Cambridge, MA: Harvard University Press.

Herman, E. (1992) Being and doing: humanistic psychology and the spirit of the 1960s, in B.L. Tischler (ed.) *Sights on the Sixties*. New Brunswick, NJ: Rutgers University Press.

Hillman, J. (1983) *Healing Fiction*. New York: Springer.

Holmes, J. (2002) All you need is cognitive behaviour therapy?, *British Medical Journal*, 324 (7332): 288–94.

Holmes, J. and Lindley, R. (1998) *The Values of Psychotherapy* (rev. edn). London: Karnac.

Hook, D. and Eagle, G. (eds) (2002) *Psychopathology and Social Prejudice*: Cape Town: UCT Press.

Hubble, M.A., Duncan, B.L. and Miller, S.D. (1999) *The Heart and Soul of Change: What Works in Therapy*. Washington, DC: American Psychological Association.

Jones, C., Shillito-Clarke, C., Syme, G. *et al.* (2000) *Questions of Ethics in Counselling and Therapy*. Buckingham: Open University Press.

Kirschenbaum, H. and Henderson, V.L. (eds) (1990) *Carl Rogers Dialogues*. London: Constable.

Lacan, J. (1977) *The Four Fundamental Concepts of Psycho-analysis*. London: Hogarth Press.

Lambert, M.J. and Bergin, A.E. (1994) The effectiveness of psychotherapy, in A.E. Bergin and S.L. Garfield (eds) *Handbook of Psychotherapy and Behaviour Change*. New York: Wiley.

Lomas, P. (1999) *Doing Good: Psychotherapy Out of its Depth*. Oxford: Oxford University Press.

Lyotard, J-F. (1984) *The Postmodern Condition: A Report on Knowledge*. Manchester: Manchester University Press.

Mace, C., Moorey, S. and Roberts, B. (2001) *Evidence in the Psychological Therapies: A Critical Guide for Practitioners*. Hove: Brunner–Routledge.

Mowbray, R. (1995) *The Case against Psychotherapy Registration: A Conservation Issue for the Human Potential Movement*. London: Trans Marginal Press.

Parker, I. (ed.) (1999) *Deconstructing Psychotherapy*. London: Sage.

Parker, I., Georgaca, E., Harper, D. *et al.* (1995) *Deconstructing Psychopathology*. London: Sage.

Polkinghorne, D.E. (1992) Postmodern epistemology of practice, in S. Kvale (ed.) *Psychology and Postmodernism*. London: Sage.

Roth, A. and Fonagy, P. (1996) *What Works for Whom: A Critical Review of Psychotherapy Research*. London: Guilford.

Sampson, E.E. (1993) *Celebrating the Other: A Dialogic Account of Human Nature*. Hemel Hempstead: Harverster Wheatsheaf.

Schön, D.A. (1987) *Educating the Reflective Practitioner*. London: Jossey-Bass.

Seligman, M.E.P. (1995) The effectiveness of psychotherapy, *American Psychologist*, 50(12): 965–74.

Smith, J.A., Harre, R. and van Langenhove, L. (eds) (1995) *Rethinking Psychology*. London: Sage.

Spinelli, E. (1989) *The Interpreted World*. London: Sage.

Spinelli, E. (2001) Counselling psychology: a hesitant hybrid or a tantalising innovation, *Counselling Psychology Review*, 16(3): 3–12.

Strawbridge, S. (1999) Counselling and psychotherapy as enabling and empowering, in C. Feltham (ed.) *Controversies in Psychotherapy and Counselling*. London: Sage.

Strawbridge, S. and Woolfe, R. (2003) Counselling psychology in context, in R. Woolfe, W. Dryden and S. Strawbridge (eds) *Handbook of Counselling Psychology*, 2nd edn. London: Sage.

Tjeltveit, A.C. (1999) *Ethics and Values in Psychotherapy*. London: Routledge.

Weber, M. (1974) *The Protestant Ethic and the Spirit of Capitalism*, trans. T. Parsons. London: Unwin University Books.

2 Ethical thinking in individual therapy

Caroline Jones

Individual therapy describes the activity that occurs when the therapist and client meet face to face in private. Key points about this modality are identified in the section on characteristics. The section on critical situations illustrates the ethical thinking that underpins this form of therapy, with its focus on client autonomy and fidelity within the therapeutic relationship. The codes of a number of professional associations in the UK embody these principles and I draw upon these in this chapter. Even the most detailed code, however, cannot cover every eventuality in individual therapy, so it is important that therapists have the skills to think through other aspects that arise in their practice and arrive at ethically based decisions. In the final section on emergent issues, a number of related points are considered. For ease of reading, the term 'therapy' is used to cover the practice of counselling, psychotherapy and counselling psychology, except at those points where specific reference to one or other of these activities indicates differences between them and is therefore helpful for clarity. Similarly, the term 'client' is used throughout although some therapists prefer the term 'patient'. I am a workplace counsellor in the Midlands of England, using an eclectic approach with clients. Therefore, this chapter tends to reflect the ethical thinking of a practitioner at the counselling end of the counselling/psychotherapy continuum.

Characteristics of individual therapy

The purpose of individual therapy is to provide 'an opportunity for the client to work towards living in a way he or she experiences as more satisfying and resourceful' (BACP 1997). Its nature involves the therapeutic relationship as the main agent of change that the practitioner has any influence on (UKAHPP 2003). It is a process with psychological, educative, philosophical, emotional, behavioural, supportive and developmental elements. It is also described as a social process (McLeod 1999). The therapeutic relationship is undertaken with the best interests of the client as paramount. This requires awareness of the possible impact of the therapy on the client's external relationships (Jacobs 1998) and an understanding of the client's social and cultural context. Individual therapy varies in duration between a few and many sessions and is practised in a range of settings, from institutional, to voluntary agency, to independent (private) practice.

Any person can practise as a therapist. It is unknown how many individual therapists practise in the UK without being a member of one of the professional associations, although some belong to the Independent Practitioners Network. However, there is now a greater public awareness that selecting a therapist who belongs to a professional association offers the availability of complaints procedures in the event of bad practice. Membership of a professional association is linked to ethical practice through its requirements of standards, namely: training, competence (including mandatory regular supervision required by some professional associations) and accountability. Additionally, some professional associations have accreditation schemes that form the stepping stones to voluntary registers.[1]

Formal training on academic courses or courses run by reputable private institutions is becoming the norm. Qualifications range from diplomas to doctorates, with an emphasis on increasingly in-depth study of theoretical approaches. Training normally includes skills training, such as Egan (2001) and Nelson-Jones (2001, 2002) and an understanding of the key theoretical approaches. There is a wealth of therapeutic literature available to therapists which includes the Counselling in Action series (Sage), plus literature on theoretical approaches, such as the Core Concepts in Therapy series (Open University Press), plus the various handbooks and readers. Literature on other aspects of therapy that provide useful background reading includes texts on ethics, (for example Bond 2000; Jones *et al.* 2000), working with difference (Kearney 1996; Lago and Thompson 1996) and research findings (for example Department of Health 2000a), and journals such as the BACP's *Counselling and Psychotherapy Research*. Lastly, literature on unhelpful or abusive therapeutic relationships is recommended as a reminder of the harmful consequences of unethical practice (see, for example, Masson 1992; Russell 1993; POPAN 1998; Sands 2000).

The client group for individual therapy includes people of all ages, male and female, from all ethnic origins, from all walks of life, single people or individuals in relationships and, of course, therapists themselves. Between them, they bring the widest range of presenting problems. These range from mental health concerns, including stress, anxiety and depression, and personal growth, existential and life event issues including personal and domestic problems, work-related problems, unemployment, loss and bereavement, relationships and family difficulties.

To summarize, ethical thinking in individual therapy is informed by external factors such as training, the setting, experience, supervision and the ethical documents of professional associations. These have evolved to reflect current thinking about good practice, drawing upon the experience of members within each professional association and from the learning that is gained from complaints. There are also the internal factors, the unique qualities of the therapist, such as their own moral values, culture, personality and levels of self-awareness, developed, for example, through journal-keeping, meditation, prayer, the arts or personal therapy.

Critical situations and their ethical resolution

A number of situations have been selected to illustrate the application of ethical thinking to particular events and circumstances that arise within individual therapy. These are grouped under two headings: non-exploitative practice and trustworthiness (process-related), and confidentiality (content-related). The privacy that is an essential element of individual therapy is also *the* factor that makes attention to non-exploitative and trustworthy practice so important. The client, who is in the more vulnerable state (Rogers 1990), is alone in the room with the therapist and it is the therapist's responsibility to act with integrity and only in the best interests of the client, with the focus on the client's autonomy.

Non-exploitative and trustworthy practice

The ethical codes of many professional associations make specific reference to the prohibition of the exploitation of clients, typically 'in view of the personal and often intense nature of the therapeutic relationship practitioners must avoid exploiting their clients financially, sexually, emotionally or in any other way' (BPS, DCoP 2001: 1.3.3). Non-exploitative and trustworthy practice is the expression in practice of the ethical principles of beneficence, non-maleficence, fidelity and autonomy in particular, and the values of integrity, impartiality and respect. It is strongly linked to the purposeful nature of the therapy from the perspective of clients, defined by their own aims and goals, which can be wide-ranging or specific. Non-exploitative and trustworthy practice is explored in the context of situations that arise in all individual therapeutic relationships, namely at the start, during and at the ending of the relationship.

Advertising for clients and contracting with clients at the start of the therapeutic relationship is a first test of the therapist's integrity. BACP (2002) has a section on probity in professional practice that covers a range of issues of contracting. COSCA (2003: Code of Practice 3.1) encourages written contracts. Providing written information about the way the therapist practices, is evidence of the therapist's integrity.

The therapist's next test of integrity is to assess whether their skills and expertise and the setting are appropriate for the task and, if not, to refer elsewhere. Encouraging clients to ask questions is important, and respecting client autonomy is demonstrated by providing information about accessible documents for clients that facilitate understanding of their undertaking and therefore enable informed consent (BACP 1991; POPAN 1998; Department of Health 2001b). In addition, informing clients of the code(s) the therapist abides by, with details of how to obtain further information on these, respects client autonomy. BASRT (1999: Code of Practice 1.8) considers this a duty. There are additional issues to consider when contracting with young people (Hamilton 2001) or those deemed unable to give informed consent (BPS, DCoP 2002: 5).

Clear contracting in independent practice includes information about fees, and the likelihood of fee increases if a long-term relationship is anticipated. Whatever the setting, therapists may wish to clarify agreements about missed sessions, how to contact clients in an emergency, contact between sessions and other 'housekeeping' matters. One vital ethical issue at the start of the relationship is to establish that it is the client's decision to seek therapy. This cannot be assumed merely on the basis that the client has turned up. The client may be responding to an 'instruction' or as a condition from a third party. Discussion about this allows the client time to decide whether to proceed and is fundamental to respecting their autonomy.

> Pauline has booked an appointment with one of the workplace counsellors and arrived for her first session. The counsellor invites her to say why she is here and Pauline describes a conflict at her work-place and mentions in passing that her line manager suggested she come for counselling. The counsellor picks upon this and asks her whether she had previously been thinking of using the counselling service to explore this conflict. Pauline says no and they discuss whether she wishes to continue. Pauline is clearly undecided and is invited to think further and contact the counsellor again if she wishes to proceed.[2]

Having established that the client is attending 'deliberately and voluntarily' (BACP 1991) or 'normally with explicit consent' (BACP 2002), the therapist has to consider whether there are any other factors to consider that may affect their delivery of an ethical service. Checking with the client whether they have been in therapy before and, if so, what were the helpful and unhelpful factors of that therapy (O'Connell 1998) assists in the building of the working alliance and the likelihood of establishing psychological contact. If there has been a previous involvement in therapy that used a different theoretical approach, modality or involved a dissimilar setting or medium, the therapist can clarify any differences in ethical practice in this modality and setting.

Dual relationships may be easily identifiable at this stage, but the possibilities of overlapping worlds or conflicts of interests may not be so apparent. The COSCA Code of Practice (2003: 6.1–2) states that the counsellor 'will not enter into a working relationship with any client about whom the member has prior knowledge which might cause a conflict of interest' and 'when a potential conflict of interest becomes apparent after the working relationship with a client has commenced, the member has a duty to acknowledge the conflict of interest to the client and seek an equitable resolution to the situation.' The UKAHPP

(2003: Code of Practice 4.4.4) states: 'Potential conflicts of interest that might arise are made clear to all parties concerned'. The BACP (2002) makes reference to conflicts of interest under the principle of autonomy: '. . . and inform the client in advance of foreseeable conflicts of interest or as soon as possible after such conflicts become apparent.' Employed therapists have to manage the conflict of interest that arises from always having more than one client – the person in the room and the organization that pays them. Maintaining impartiality, such as declining an advocacy role on behalf of clients in the event of their involvement in complaints and disciplinary procedures, is one way to manage this conflict of interest. Institutions themselves can also assist towards the avoidance of overlapping worlds or other conflicts of interest by the way they manage their referral systems.

Dual relationships are the subject of growing attention in therapy literature (Wosket 1999; Shillito-Clarke 2000a; Lazarus and Zur 2002; Syme 2003). Workplace therapists have a dual relationship with all clients in that both therapist and client are employees. Those clients who consider this a problem seek therapy help elsewhere; others may see this as serving to 'democratise and humanise therapeutic relationships and divest them of unnecessary trappings of paternalism, hierarchy and mystery (Wosket 1999: 145). The BACP (2002: Guidance 4) encourages practitioners 'to consider the implications of entering into dual relationships with clients, to avoid entering into relationships that are likely to be detrimental to clients'.

All therapists also have to manage those situations where they have met, either in the context of therapy or in more public arenas, others connected to the client's world. The longer the therapist has worked in an institution, the more likely it is that this will occur. When worlds overlap, focusing only on the client's perceptions and experiences is a basic skill of therapy, although working simultaneously with individuals who know one another is probably unwise. However successfully the therapist has maintained boundaries in their mind about the two clients, the value of the work could be undermined if the clients discovered that they were both seeing the same therapist at the same time. There is an obligation on the therapist to act with both in ways that do not undermine their faith in therapy as a means of helping. Clear contracting can still result in ethical dilemmas.

Having understood the motives and goals of each client, the counsellors decide how to use their theoretical approach(es) and skills to greatest effect. At the same time, therapists remain humble in the knowledge that as much as 40 per cent of 'improvement' depends on client variables and extra-therapeutic factors (see Chapter 1). Depending on the problems brought, it may be appropriate to alert the client to the possibility that they may feel worse before feeling better. Confidence in the theoretical approach used is an important but not the only factor. Murdin (2001: 117) comments that 'sometimes the achievements of psychotherapy are brought about by the charismatic force of the therapist's personality and faith and sometimes by a very routine application of well-known and tested methods.'

Therapists have an ethical and moral responsibility to be trustworthy within the therapeutic relationship (fidelity). This applies both to the content of the work (explored later in this chapter), and to the ways in which the therapy is conducted such as the therapist's behaviour, attitudes, interventions and pace of the work. Therapy, however, is not a science, and while best practice may be the goal with every client, 'good enough' is the more realistic hope. Therapists can make mistakes and errors of judgement, and ideally the therapeutic relationship is strong enough for these to be acknowledged and put right (Palmer Barnes 1998; Casemore 1999).

Another important example of trustworthiness is the establishment of proper boundaries, including the prohibition of sexual activity between therapist and client. Typically, the BACP (2002: Guidance 18) states: 'sexual relations with clients are prohibited. "Sexual relations" include intercourse, any other type of sexual activity or sexualised behaviour.' Shillito-Clarke (2000b: 146) comments that, 'the reason "sexual activity" is hard to define is that it is a social construct: a set of behaviours and attributes that a group of people have agreed to classify and label.' It is the therapist's responsibility not to initiate any form of sexual activity and the therapist's responsibility to explain why such activity is inappropriate if the client initiates this. Sexual feelings may be present in the therapy room and the therapist works with these as required.

Trustworthiness includes obvious features such as therapist punctuality and reliability, and less measurable factors such as the therapist's ability to 'contain' the client's material.

> Tom is an experienced therapist who had survived a serious train crash some years before. When Sonia came for counselling following a car crash, in which her partner was killed, Tom found

he was unexpectedly re-experiencing his own feelings of survivor guilt after their sessions. Discussion in supervision enabled him to consider referral on to another therapist when Tom acknowledged that his own feelings were too close to the surface to hear Sonia's unique experience. Tom was not troubled by this in his work with other clients bringing equally demanding but unrelated material.

Trustworthiness includes many other elements of practice including:

- working in a non-oppressive way with clients;
- monitoring functioning, physical and emotional well-being;
- attending to feedback, direct and inferred, from clients and in supervision;
- attending to relevant continuing professional development.

There is limited reference to endings and the link between this phase of therapy to the principles of beneficence and non-maleficence in the codes, although it is at this point that there are further potential dangers of exploitation. Keeping clients beyond the usefulness of the therapy or ending the therapy suddenly are both harmful to the client (UKAHPP 2003: 4.5). The theoretical approach and the setting of the therapist influence the management of endings. In solution-focused or brief therapy, there is an inbuilt expectation by both parties that sessions are limited in number. Open-ended therapy varies in duration between a few or many sessions, with the expectation that the longer the therapy has lasted, the longer the ending phase will be. Institutional settings, such as workplace services, employee assistance programmes (EAPs) and primary care services, often set limits on the number of sessions available to clients in order to enable access to the service by as many people as possible. This requires an approach to endings that acknowledges from the start that the limited number of sessions affects the scope of the therapy. Clients and therapists share the responsibility of how best to utilize the time available to them.

Endings may occur unexpectedly when clients stop coming quite suddenly because of the difficulties that can arise when contemplating endings or because they have had enough or because the therapy is not meeting their needs. This occasions an ethical dilemma for therapists: should they contact the client to discuss this or not? As each relationship is unique, the principles of beneficence, non-maleficence, autonomy and value of respect require consideration (Syme 2000). Similar dilemmas occur for therapists when they consider it appropriate to bring the work to an end because it is no longer helpful to the client, or when therapy itself maintains the status quo and becomes a barrier to the client's growth. Here, the therapist's professional responsibility conflicts with the client's wishes.

During the ending phase of therapy, attention to the future boundaries is necessary so that clients understand that the ending of therapy is not likely to lead to the start of another kind of relationship. The duty of care that therapists hold does not cease when therapy ends. The UKAHPP (2003: Code of Practice 4.4.3) clearly states: 'Non-professional relationships with former clients are avoided whenever possible'. The BACP (2002: Guidance 18) takes the view that 'practitioners should think carefully about, and exercise considerable caution before, entering into personal or business relationships with former clients and should expect to be professionally accountable if the relationship becomes detrimental to the client or the standing of the profession.'

Occasionally, endings can result in unexpected consequences for the therapist. Hudson-Allez (2002) reports on research into the incidence of therapists receiving unwanted attentions from former clients. These can range from directly intrusive behaviours such as gifts, letters, persistent telephone calls and (the more threatening) stalking, to indirect harassment by the unwarranted use of complaints procedures. Taking action to put a stop to such incidents can be a dilemma for therapists as reporting such behaviour may involve a breach of confidentiality. Normally, the identity of clients is confidential.

Confidentiality

Confidentiality is considered both a principle and a value of therapy. Effectiveness requires that individual therapy is highly confidential – that is, between therapist and client – though discussed, in an anonymous and respectful way, in the supervisory relationship. Limits to confidentiality are those instances where the law (Bond 1999, 2001, 2003; Jones 2000a) or where additional constraints of settings apply, or when during the therapy there may be a conflict between the principle of autonomy and the public interest if the client intends serious harm to self or others.

Codes vary in the wordings about the law: therapists are bound either to work within the law (COSCA Statement of Ethics 2003: 2.8) or to be aware of the law (BPS, DCoP 2001: 1.6). Demands from outside the therapy room that challenge the confidentiality of the therapeutic process can arise when therapists work as part of a team in, for example, a medical setting. In these circumstances, it is essential when contracting with clients to clarify the limits to confidentiality, to explain when and why client information is to be shared with other professionals and to obtain informed consent. Useful guidance in these circumstances, and in relation to record-keeping, is available (BPS, DCoP 2002). Record-keeping is an aspect of practice that clients have a *right* to know about and, where records exist, they have a right of access to them on request. The decision whether or not to keep records is an idiosyncratic one (Jacobs 2002) and an ethical one. The BACP (2002: Guidance 5) suggests that records should be kept unless there are adequate reasons not to. The question for each therapist is, 'Why keep these?' The existence of records may be assumed by third parties who in certain circumstances make requests for access to them.

Writing a report, or reference, at the request of the client, can be requested of therapists irrespective of setting. Confidentiality within the therapeutic relationship is an important consideration, supported by the BACP definition of fidelity, which includes 'restricting any disclosure of confidential information about clients to furthering the purposes for which it was originally disclosed' (2002: 3). Other ethical concerns include:

- Integrity: should the therapist produce a report if the whole picture available to them undermines the client in some way? To be selective with the client's material calls into question the therapist's impartiality.
- Purposefulness: to be involved in matters outside the therapy room distorts the purpose of individual therapy which is concerned with the way the client feels, thinks, behaves and relates to others.

Other than the therapeutic gains that clients proceed to use to their own benefit, clients should be neither advantaged nor disadvantaged by their choice to enter therapy.

Confidentiality is tested on those occasions when the client is at risk of harm from others or causing harm to others. The BACP (2002: Guidance 14) describes these as

> situations in which the practitioner should be alert to the possibility of conflicting responsibilities between those concerning their client, other people who may be significantly affected, and society generally. . . . In all cases, the aim should be to ensure for the client a good quality of care that is as respectful of the client's capacity for self-determination and their trust as circumstances permit.

Situations of this nature cannot be legislated for in codes since, as with all dilemmas, each case is unique. On these occasions, the values and personal moral qualities of the therapist are the guiding factors when deciding which course of action does the greatest good and least harm to the client and others. Familiarity with risk assessment is helpful in these situations (Morgan 1998; Reeves 2001). Supervision, the forum to discuss and weigh up the risks, is helpful and, if not available at short notice, then consultation with another experienced practitioner is recommended. Individual therapy provides clients with the opportunity to talk unreservedly about their thoughts and feelings and is where they can expect a respectful and empathic response. Ideally, in these circumstances, disclosure to third parties is a dilemma that is shared between therapist and client, covering what needs to be shared, with whom and by whom.

> Asif becomes increasingly angry during the course of his counselling. He sometimes speaks of his frustration at the slowness of his managers to deal with his complaint of racial harassment and his despair at this ever being resolved. His feelings sometimes veer towards thoughts of harming his colleagues and sometimes towards thoughts of suicide. The counsellor takes this to supervision, where risk assessment is undertaken regularly. Having her own fears contained in supervision enables the counsellor in turn to contain Asif's strong feelings. She decides to wait. The employer upholds the complaint and this enables Asif to have some confidence in the future. His violent and suicidal feelings rapidly subside and the counselling comes to end after a few more sessions.

Another challenge to confidentiality occurs when therapists are approached in connection with civil or criminal proceedings (Jones 2000b). Hudson-Allez (2001) describes the steps taken to avoid handing over case notes, arguing professional and legal grounds (Human Rights Act 2000, Article 8). Individual therapists may also work as trainers, or in research or write for publication. On the occasions that they draw on client material and their own experiences as therapists, an issue to consider is that of consent by clients. Again, this is a matter that can be covered in the therapist's initial written information for clients.

To summarize, critical situations in individual therapy are not only the unforeseeable ethical dilemmas that arise occasionally but also the regular features arising in every therapeutic encounter. These include the exchange of information, the clarification of expectations, the avoidance of obvious pitfalls, the establishment and eventual ending of a purposeful, productive and safe working alliance. The professional associations have codified their collective experience about these aspects to offer guidance and instructions on the most beneficial and least harmful ways to undertake this process.

Emergent issues in ethical practice

It seems that there is a price to pay for the greater acceptance of the usefulness of individual therapy, an aim that the BACP has worked hard to achieve. The increase in accessible therapy, particularly through its provision in college, workplace/EAP and surgery settings, is clearly beneficial. This has enabled a wide range of people to access therapy services free at the point of contact, with benefits in return for the providers. There can be unexpected consequences arising from this increased provision, however. Recent case law has established, for example, that the provision of counselling services by employers defends them against claims by employees for stress as claimants need to prove that they have suffered recognizable psychological harm *and* that the employer has been in breach of their duty. Where an employer has provided appropriate counselling services they are unlikely to be found in breach of duty (Dyer 2002). This changes the nature of the relationship between employers and workplace therapists, whose very existence now offers the employer protection against stress claims unless psychological harm can be proved. In another way, dilemmas also exist for therapists with contracts with some EAPs, where referrals may depend on compliance with record-keeping that may diminish therapeutic confidentiality.

Demands upon any therapist to disclose the content of therapy to third parties, albeit with the consent of clients, include requests from solicitors for reports or for access to client case notes in order to further claims for compensation after accidents and disasters or in cases taken to tribunals. This conflicts with the purpose of therapy as identified at the start of this chapter: to experience more satisfying and resourceful ways of being. Clients now need to be warned that there is a possibility that access to their therapy records could be sought at some future date in connection with events occurring long after the therapy has ended. The privacy that individual therapy offers could come even more under threat through future legislation. Currently, for example, drug trafficking legislation requires disclosure of knowledge or suspicion of drug money laundering, placing therapists in an informant role. Professional associations need to be campaigning for the privilege of confidentiality allowed to lawyers, rather than leaving this to be argued, case by case, by courageous therapists. Safeguarding the nature and purpose of individual therapy and its principles and values requires constant vigilance.

Membership of a professional association by individual therapists currently offers clients quality assurance. If statutory regulation of therapists occurs, will this be more beneficial for clients? Statutory regulation would confer the protection of title for counsellors and psychotherapists using powers under the Health Act 1999 (Richardson 2002). Chartered counselling and clinical psychologists already have this protection. It appears that the drive towards statutory regulation is either viewed as inevitable by the professional associations or actively sought by them despite resistance from within their memberships and others (House and Totton 1997; Thorne 2002).

To assist therapists with the new demands that arise from outside the therapy room, documents such the BACP's *Ethical Framework for Good Practice in Counselling and Psychotherapy* (2002) offer the principles and values to consider when making decisions in practice. The personal moral qualities that practitioners are strongly encouraged to aspire to are particularly relevant to the individual therapist working alone with their clients. Additionally, this document accommodates different philosophies, alternative theoretical approaches, various settings and modalities, as well as the life experience and cultural heritage of the practitioner.

In conclusion, individual therapy is well established as a form of helping, there is a respectable body of research to confirm its effectiveness, and it is more widely available today than ever before. I believe that the road to making therapy more professional in terms of standards has become blurred with the route to establishing therapy as a profession. The prospect of statutory regulation exists. Increasing threats to confidentiality exist. These matters are probably the most important ethical challenges faced by individual therapists and need to be resolved collectively by considering what is in the best interests of all concerned – clients, therapists and in the society where it is practised.

Notes

1. Such as: the United Kingdom Register of Counsellors, which includes more than 2500 members of BACP, UKAHPP and COSCA; the National Register of Psychotherapists, which includes 5100 members from 80 member organizations of UKCP such as UKAHPP and BASRT; and the BCP Register, which includes over 1400 psychoanalysts, analytical psychologists, psychoanalytic psychotherapists and child psychotherapists from member societies, including BAP. Some individual therapists are on more than one register. At the time of writing, BACP had over 20,000 individual members.
2. The vignettes in this chapter are fictional, drawing upon my casework experience.

References

BACP (1991) *Basic Principles of Counselling*. Rugby: British Association for Counselling and Psychotherapy.

BACP (1997) *Code of Ethics and Practice for Counsellors*. Rugby: British Association for Counselling and Psychotherapy.

BACP (2002) *Ethical Framework for Good Practice in Counselling and Psychotherapy*. Rugby: British Association for Counselling and Psychotherapy.

BASRT (1999) *Code of Ethics* and *Code of Practice*. London: British Association for Sexual and Relationship Therapy (first published 1996).

Bond, T. (1999) *Confidentiality: Counselling and the Law*. Rugby: British Association for Counselling and Psychotherapy.

Bond, T. (2000) *Standards and Ethics for Counselling in Action*, 2nd edn. London: Sage.

Bond, T. (2001) *Confidentiality: Counselling and the Law in Scotland*. Rugby: British Association for Counselling and Psychotherapy.

Bond, T. (2003) *Confidentiality Matters* (provisional title). London: Sage.

BPS, DCoP (2001) *Professional Practice Guidelines*. Leicester: British Psychological Society.

BPS, DCoP (2002) *Guidelines on Confidentiality and Record Keeping*. Leicester: British Psychological Society.

Casemore, R. (1999) Why can't we own our mistakes? *Counselling*, 10(2): 94–5.

COSCA (2003) *Statement of Ethics and Code of Practice*. Stirling: Confederation of Scottish Counselling Agencies.

Department of Health (2001a) *Treatment Choice in Psychological Therapies and Counselling*. London: DH Publications.

Department of Health (2001b) *Choosing Talking Therapies*. London: DH Publications.

Dyer, C. (2002) Considering counselling, *Health and Safety Bulletin*, July: 11–20.

Egan, G. (2001) *The Skilled Helper*, 7th edn. Monterey, CA: Brooks/Cole.

Hamilton, C. (2001) *Offering Children Confidentiality: Law and Guidance*. Colchester: University of Essex, Children's Legal Centre.

House, R. and Totton N. (eds) (1997) *Implausible Professions: Arguments for Pluralism and Autonomy in Psychotherapy and Counselling*. Ross-on-Wye: PCCS Books.

Hudson-Allez, G. (2001) Judge rules against confidentiality agreements, *CPC Review*, 2(1): 1.

Hudson-Allez, G. (2002) The prevalence of stalking of psychological therapists working in primary care by current or former clients, *Counselling and Psychotherapy Research* 2(2): 139–46.

Jacobs, M. (1998) *The Presenting Past*, 2nd edn. Buckingham: Open University Press.

Jacobs, M. (2002) Research on case notes, *Counselling and Psychotherapy Journal*, 13(3): 6–8.

Jones, C., Shillito-Clarke, C., Syme, G. *et al.* (2000) *Questions of Ethics in Counselling and Therapy*. Buckingham: Open University Press.

Jones, C. (2000a) Ethical counselling is properly described as highly confidential. What are some of the limits to complete confidentiality with a counselling relationship?, in C. Jones, C. Shillito-Clarke, G. Syme, *et al. Questions of Ethics in Counselling and Therapy*. Buckingham: Open University Press.

Jones, C. (2000b) What should counsellors consider when contacted by persons such as solicitors or the police or other authorities in connection with client work or when clients request this?, in C. Jones, C. Shillito-Clarke, G. Syme, *et al. Questions of Ethics in Counselling and Therapy*. Buckingham: Open University Press.

Kearney, A. (1996) *Counselling, Class and Politics*. Manchester: PCCS Books.

Lago, C. and Thompson, J. (1996) *Race, Culture and Counselling*. Buckingham: Open University Press.

Lazarus, A. and Zur, O. (eds) (2002) *Dual Relationships and Psychotherapy*. New York: Springer.

Masson, G. (1992) *Against Therapy*. London: HarperCollins.

McLeod, J. (1999) Counselling as a social process, *Counselling*, 10(3): 217–22.

Morgan, S. (1998) *Assessing and Managing Risk*. Brighton: Pavilion.

Murdin, L. (2001) *How Much is Enough? Endings in Psychotherapy and Counselling*. London: Routledge.

Nelson-Jones, R. (2001) *Introduction to Counselling Skills: Text and Activities*. London: Sage.

Nelson-Jones, R. (2002) *Essential Counselling and Therapy Skills: Using the Skilled Client Model*. London: Sage.

O'Connell, B (1998) *Solution-focused Therapy*. London: Sage.

Palmer Barnes, F. (1998) *Complaints and Grievances in Psychotherapy: A Handbook of Ethical Practice*. London: Routledge.

POPAN (1998) *What To Look For When You Go Into Therapy*. London: Prevention of Professional Abuse Network.

Reeves, A. (2001) Assessing risk, *Counselling*, 12(8): 36–7.

Richardson, A. (2002) Setting standards, *Counselling and Psychotherapy Journal*, 13(1): 4–5.

Rogers, C. (1990) A theory of therapy, personality, and interpersonal relationships, as developed in the client-centred framework, in H. Kirchenbaum and V.L. Henderson (eds) *The Carl Rogers Reader*. London: Constable.

Russell J. (1993) *Out of Bounds: Sexual Exploitation in Counselling and Therapy*. London: Sage.

Sands, A. (2000) *Falling for Therapy: Psychotherapy from a Client's Point of View*. London: Palgrave.

Shillito-Clarke, C. (2000a) What are the arguments for and against avoidable dual relationships such as being a counsellor and a trainer, a trainer and a supervisor or a supervisor to a work colleague who is also a friend?, in C. Jones, C. Shillito-Clark, G. Syme, *et al. Questions of Ethics in Counselling and Therapy*. Buckingham: Open University Press.

Shillito-Clarke, C. (2000b) Sex or sexual activity with a client, trainee or supervisee is unethical in our profession but what constitutes sexual activity in a counselling, training or supervisory relationship?, in C. Jones, C. Shillito-Clark, G. Syme, *et al. Questions of Ethics in Counselling and Therapy*. Buckingham: Open University Press.

Syme, G. (2000) The client fails to come to the next session – do you contact the client? How might the setting of the counselling also influence the decision?, in C. Jones, C. Shillito-Clark, G. Syme, *et al.* (eds) *Questions of Ethics in Counselling and Therapy*. Buckingham: Open University Press.

Syme, G. (2003) *Dual Relationships in Counselling and Psychotherapy: Exploring the Limits*. London: Sage.

Thorne, B. (2002) Regulation – a treacherous path? *Counselling and Psychotherapy Journal*, 13(2): 4–5.

UKAHPP (2003) UKAHPP Core Beliefs and Practice, UKAHPP Code of Ethical Principles, UKAHPP Ethical Review Procedure and UKAHPP Code of Practice, in *Handbook and National Membership Register*. London: United Kingdom Association of Humanistic Psychology Practitioners.

Wosket, V. (1999) *The Therapeutic Use of Self: Counselling Practice, Research and Supervision*. London: Routledge.

3 Telephone work, with special reference to Samaritans

Joan Guénault

'But what good is it on the telephone?' The question of the efficacy of providing emotional support by telephone, be it within a counselling service or the use of counselling skills in a different context such as Samaritans, is the first ethical question that practitioners in this field must pose to themselves. At least part of the answer is supplied by a look at the growth in the number and use of telephone helplines. Although the Samaritan service is not specifically a helpline, the vast majority of contacts are made by telephone. When, however, the service began in the early 1950s the idea of support by telephone was revolutionary, even though it was initially only part of a broader picture of 'drop-in' access, possibly after a first contact by telephone. Many years later, serious doubts were expressed in some quarters about just how effective telephone contact alone could be for the caller. Yet the *Guidelines for Good Practice* (Telephone Helplines Association 1999: 11) point out that over a thousand helplines then existed in the UK, and in 2001 Samaritans alone received in excess of 4 million calls. In addition, ad hoc lines set up for a short timespan and a particular purpose, such as after a harrowing television programme, are now a familiar feature of our society.

Characteristics of telephone work

It is clear that emotional support offered by telephone has become widely accepted as valid. There are, however, aspects of ethics that particularly apply to this area of work, and these in their turn have an impact firstly on the recruitment and selection of practitioners and subsequently on the support and training needed by them. Recruitment publicity must give an accurate impression of what is involved in the work, not always easy to achieve in a punchy and succinct way. Moreover, this must be done in a manner that does not deter potential clients from using the service. For instance, very depressed callers can often think themselves unworthy of anyone's attention, so it is not uncommon for a Samaritan volunteer responding to such a caller to hear something like, 'I shouldn't be ringing, you must have much more deserving people trying to get through.' An advertisement that portrays the service as about to collapse under the strain because of a shortage of practitioners may be successful in generating more offers of help, but it might also deter such a caller from ringing. This is unacceptable: a middle way must be found.

What, then, is the next step? Samaritans has mounted its recruitment campaign and willing helpers have applied. What should they reasonably expect to happen now? Firstly, they should receive fuller information than is possible in a brief item of publicity; information that enables them to assess whether, in terms of the practical requirements, it is worth their taking their interest further. After this stage, however, there is a divergence of approach. Some services move people on to training, with little or no selection beforehand; others operate a thorough pre-training selection process. Samaritans falls into the latter category, taking the view that this is good practice for both those who proceed further and those who do not. Those for whom the work is not a good fit to their values, attitudes and basic abilities should be enabled to discover this without committing themselves to the time and effort of the training programme. On the other hand, those for whom the fit is good should be freed from the sense of assessment during training so that they can open themselves to fulfilling their own personal learning and development needs.

The selection process itself, then, must give a good feel for the demands of the work in personal terms. While interviews make a useful contribution to this, there is a need to supplement them with group activities. Together, these two elements can give both the selectors and the applicant an accurate impression of whether, with training, this person could become competent in the work and comfortable with the way the organization operates. The effectiveness of selection is enhanced by including activities which translate the organization's values and principles into typical situations requiring example responses in a group situation. This is especially true of the more extreme situations which may occasionally have to be faced, such as respecting someone's right to die if they have made that deliberate choice, and of situations that raise issues on which people often have strong views, such as the rights and wrongs of abortion. In a group, differences of opinion will arise, requiring discussion and negotiation. Participants themselves become more aware of their own instinctive reactions, and selectors can observe these more easily. It is important, however, that judgements are, as far as possible, made according to objective criteria rather than subjective impressions, and that where subjective impressions have a necessary contribution to make then the opinions of more than one selector are taken into account.

Once selected, a typical Samaritan volunteer participates in a series of preparatory training sessions exploring appropriate theoretical background and experiential work, followed by a mentored probationary period and further training throughout their membership. As a consequence of the high proportion of telephone contacts, these activities must all give special emphasis to this element of the work. For example, effective use of the voice assumes even more importance than in a face-to-face situation. Rosenfield (1997: 93) points out that, 'How the counsellor actually sounds can have a big impact on how the client responds', and goes on to identify research conducted on the effects of counsellor vocal quality. In addition, whether by vocal quality or choice of words, and usually by both, the practitioner must be able to convey those aspects of, for instance, empathy and acceptance which in a face-to-face situation are experienced visually. Sanders (1993) provides some useful practical pointers. In Samaritan work, the telephone is also used as a support tool for volunteers, providing them with access to immediate help at all times, and enabling prompt debriefing at the end of a duty shift.

Critical situations and their ethical resolution

Callers are of all ages, and come from all backgrounds and walks of life. The common feature is that they make contact when experiencing a distress-inducing situation, maybe even despairing to the point of considering suicide. The situations presented consequently cover the whole range of those which might cause any of us emotional difficulty. The approach adopted in Samaritans' telephone work, as in all their work, is that of 'the listening therapy' as developed by the founder of the organization. The validity of this approach as an element of emotional support in even the most extreme of personal crises is endorsed in *Suicide Prevention: The Challenge Confronted* (Morgan and Williams 1994: 23), for example with the statement that, 'To reach out and listen is itself the first major step in reducing the level of suicidal despair.' Although developed independently, the Samaritan approach of active listening is closely akin to a Rogerian non-directive person-centred approach. It is embodied in its set of *Seven Principles and Practices* (Samaritans 1981) which are in effect the organization's ethical code. These were complemented in 2001 by its *Mission, Vision and Values* statement (see Appendix 2 of this book). These statements give a central position to the need to be accessible at the moment of deepest personal crisis, a need corroborated by leading professionals in the field of suicide research. For instance, Shneidman (1985: 234) as quoted in Eldrid (1988: 147) says: 'A highly suicidal state is characterized by its transient quality, its pervasive ambivalence, and its dyadic nature.' Eldrid himself goes on to draw the inference that 'the immediate need then is to be available, to listen with sensitivity and patience'. Callers are sometimes drawing on other sources of help while also looking to Samaritans for emotional support: but in the middle of the night when the emotional need may be greatest most helping agencies are unavailable. Thus Samaritans consider the 24-hour, every day of the year, aspect of their service to be a crucial element of their accessibility. Enabling this level of availability points to the telephone as one obvious means of contact.

Whatever the time of day or night, the possibility of immediate access created by this mode of contact is one example of a shift in the 'balance of power' in favour of the caller. There are others. Calls can not only be made at the caller's preferred time, but also can easily be terminated when the caller should choose. This might even be before the caller has spoken, if, for instance, having plucked up the courage to ring and talk about debilitating difficulties, on connection they find that these problems for the moment defy expression. The person receiving such a call may succeed in enabling the caller to stay on the line until they find the words they need, but it is still in the caller's gift to end the call as soon as it becomes too taxing to continue. Such a withdrawal is not so easily achieved in a face-to-face situation, where the equivalent would be physically to walk out abruptly and maybe without even speaking: an act requiring considerable conviction just when such conviction is likely to be in short supply.

Perhaps less obviously there may a subtle shift in a caller's perception of their status in relation to that of the practitioner they are ringing. They have no visual clues as to, for instance, social standing or ethnic background. They have not had to visit an office or counselling room but merely to pick up the telephone and dial, something they do routinely. It must be acknowledged that the particular act of ringing a support service for help may feel anything but routine to the caller, but it is assuredly closer to normal everyday operations than finding one's way to an unfamiliar place for an appointment with a person as yet unknown. Rosenfield (1997: 101) identifies a number of advantages of telephone counselling as compared with face-to-face counselling, among which she lists: 'There is greater equality between the client and counsellor as the relationship develops.' This is undoubtedly a possibility, and may be so from the very start. Experience indicates that there is an earlier readiness on the part of the caller to identify and explore deep and very personal emotions in a telephone contact, and a sense of greater equality may contribute to this. Indeed, Samaritans underline in their own minds this equality between themselves and those contacting them by using the terminology of 'caller' rather than 'client', whether the contact is by telephone or by some other means.

Another enabling feature of the telephone is that access to the service by this mode is easier for many of those for whom travelling is a problem, for example because of geographical isolation or personal mobility difficulties. Also, with additional equipment, text-phone services can be provided for those with hearing impairment, and email access for anyone who finds this preferable for whatever reason to a personal visit (email services are considered in more detail in Chapter 4).

However, together with the advantages for the caller embodied in the telephone as a mode of contact, there can be disadvantages. The delicate balance for some callers between receiving adequate support and developing an overdependence on the service is even more of a dilemma in an access-on-demand situation, and it is important that the service provider does not collude in generating an unhelpful dependence. It is all too easy to be drawn into a kind of parallel universe in which the caller operates in an artificial world of uncritical acceptance and warmth of response, to the exclusion of real-world relationships. Practitioners should always make clear, whether explicitly or implicitly, what type and extent of support the organization can offer the caller, and publicity for the service should be congruent with this so that an unambiguous message is communicated.

Nevertheless, even if all this is consistently achieved, there will inevitably still be situations where a caller asks more than the service is intended to offer. In such circumstances it may be necessary to consider how they might limit their calls. Ideally any limitation on extent of contact would be implemented only with the caller's full agreement after consultation, and their subsequent cooperation. In practice this will not always be possible, and then the walking of this particular tightrope in the best interests of the caller becomes not only more difficult but also an act for which a good safety net must first be put in place. The net needs to be there for both caller and agency. If the caller 'falls off', plans for alternative support must already be in place. So if a caller's frequency or length of contact is to be limited, practitioners must be able to adjust these limitations if the caller's circumstances change in a way which indicates that they need fuller support. If the organization 'falls off', through, for example, some adverse publicity suggesting they are not offering what they promise, plans need to be already in place for ensuring that this will not deter other callers who need the service, from using it.

The limiting of calls is thrown into sharpest relief in situations where callers not merely overuse the service but palpably misuse it. In order to protect its service for those who properly need it and to enable practitioners to be undistracted in continuing to offer that service, an agency must take a firm line on abuse of this sort. Policies on dealing with sexually demanding calls and abusive callers, and training to give confidence in implementing these policies, are essential if those offering emotional support on the telephone lines are to be able to react appropriately to those other callers who need it. Full expression of the feelings of practitioners in response to receiving such a call must be encouraged in debriefing and through further support mechanisms. Feelings of having been 'used' in an unpleasant sense are often voiced. If, in addition, the policy is that in normal circumstances a call comes to an end by mutual agreement but in these circumstances the person receiving the call may put the telephone down first without any such agreement, there may be an extra element of feelings of guilt or failure. A pragmatic consequence of neglecting these complex reactions may be loss of a good practitioner to the service, but equally importantly the support given in this way can be seen as an ethical yardstick in the agency's care for its workers.

Confidentiality is a key element of many support services, and certainly of any service adhering to the BACP *Ethical Framework* (2002) or the Telephone Helplines Association's *Guidelines for Good Practice* (1999). In many respects, upholding confidentiality on the telephone is little different from other modalities, but there are instances where careful thought is needed to ensure that the ever-increasing availability of technical information does not encroach. If anonymity is also on offer to the caller, this danger becomes even more acute. For this reason, Samaritans' publicity makes it clear that the facility for caller line identification (CLI) is not used on their telephones. But is the situation so clear in relation to the tracing or tracking of calls?

Certainly these facilities are not directly available to an individual organization, but if considered justified by the appropriate authority they can be undertaken on their behalf. For instance, continued abuse of the service by a particular caller, especially if to the extent that it is interfering with the ability of others to get through on the lines, may in extreme circumstances lead to the need to enlist aid in tracking the calls in order to block further access. Such a move will normally meet with approval within the organization. But consider a different scenario: a 14-year-old girl reveals a situation of abuse by her father but insists that she wants only to be able to talk about it to someone who will respect her anonymity. She is well aware of the possible consequences of its reaching the ears of authority in whatever guise, and in spite of the situation is desperate not to break up the family. She loves her father dearly, she just wishes this particular activity would stop.

Should this call be tracked in order to identify the perpetrator and 'rescue' the girl from further abuse? The Samaritan view would be that other avenues are open to her if this is indeed what she wishes, and her awareness of these avenues and their possible consequences would be explored with her. The role of this particular service which she has chosen to ring is primarily to enable her to explore her feelings about the situation and to underpin her emotional strength to pursue whatever course of action she decides upon, even if that is to continue in the same situation. So there would be no attempt to track the source of such a call, but it must be acknowledged that acceptance of this state of affairs will not come easily to all who might be involved. Again the value of immediate support mechanisms is underlined.

This situation would become all the more acute if the caller were the perpetrator himself, the girl's father. Is not a refusal to track the source of his call tantamount to condoning his actions? There is a distinction to be drawn here between accepting the person and excusing the deed. Where confidential emotional support is what is on offer, a question that must be asked is why he chose to ring. Does he need a safe place to disentangle his confused feelings of disgust at what he is doing combined with a present inability to change his behaviour? Might this lead him to the point where change is possible? There have certainly been instances where it seems that without this emotional safety valve the inner conflict has led to suicide. And lest we are drawn into thinking at this point that this may be no bad thing, remember that his daughter loves him dearly and wants only a change in this particular aspect of his behaviour.

There are no easy answers to the ethical questions raised by circumstances similar to these, and different agencies might take different courses of action. Whatever the stance taken, it should be made very clear in preparatory training so that practitioners can be sure, before taking up the work, that they can subscribe to the organization's view and that they will receive appropriate support in such emotionally demanding circumstances.

Consider another example: a caller rings during the act of attempting suicide by taking an overdose. She does not wish any intervention, simply to be in touch with another person while she continues taking the pills, so refuses to give any identifying information. The call looks set to continue for some time, presenting a dilemma. Should the call be traced so that medical assistance might reach her before it is too late? Had this scenario arisen in a face-to-face contact the law seems clear that should she appear to lose the ability to make an informed decision for herself then the accompanying person must summon medical help. Samaritans, as most if not all other helping organizations, would act within the requirements of the law in this or indeed any situation, but it would be made clear to the caller while she was still able to understand that this is what would happen. The legal intricacies of attempted suicide by a client in the presence of a counsellor, and their implications, are well discussed by Bond (1993: 88–90).

How, though, should one react on the telephone, where the legal requirements are less well defined? The Samaritan would explain to the woman that should she become apparently unable to make her own informed decisions then the onus of responsibility would pass to Samaritans. If her informed decision is then to end the call having refused to give any information as to her whereabouts, no action would be taken. If she continues the call and appears to become unconscious with the line still open, then it may be that some effort would be made to trace her. It is in circumstances such as these that immediate and comprehensive consultation and support structures come into their own. The individual practitioner should not be expected to make decisions alone.

Again it should be noted that not all agencies will necessarily follow the same policy in all its particulars, but whatever the policy it should be clear, and an accessible and effective support structure for practitioners in situations as demanding as these should be seen as an essential and recognized feature. Indeed it could be argued that these are ethical requirements in their own right if practitioners are to be asked to deal with such situations, however rare they may be.

There are instances where the reporting of calls is required by law, and compliance with the minimum requirements should be an accepted practice. The most obvious example of this in telephone work is that of the bomb warning. There is, in any case, no breach of confidentiality here since the caller is actually intending that the message be passed on and is using the anonymity of a telephone call as a vehicle for the message. Police guidance on the procedures to be followed is clear.

Less clear-cut is implementation of the legal requirements for reporting information about threatened terrorist activities of other types. The law is unequivocal that such information must be reported. The difficulty arises in interpreting what constitutes genuine information. In such circumstances an easy and immediately accessible route to consultation with those in the organization with experience in these matters is vital. Decisions cannot reasonably be expected of the worker who receives the call, although an awareness of what detail should be elicited if possible and noted for those responsible should have been a part of their training.

Sometimes callers will 'confess' to crimes and illegalities of a non-terrorist nature. It is usually impossible for the person receiving such a call to be sure whether or not the situation as recounted is true and accurate. Reporting of such information is not required by law. In the handling of a call like this, the question of why did the caller choose to ring a service offering emotional support is again a helpful one in assessing how to respond. The caller's intention may range from simply a desire to shock, through to a genuine rehearsal of a confession before making it in a more obviously relevant forum. Eldrid (1988: 231) points out: 'It is quite surprising that although the husband who has run away from his wife and firm, often stealing large sums of his firm's money, initially is adamant about not talking to his wife, after realistic discussion he may allow you to begin some negotiations with her. The likely result is that two people's distress may be greatly reduced and the way opened for much more positive reactions.'

Acceptance of the person while not necessarily condoning actions past or present again comes to the fore in offering emotional support to prisoners. The need for this support is highlighted by official suicide statistics which indicate a significantly higher suicide rate among prisoners than in the general population. Samaritans are now welcomed throughout the prison service, sometimes directly offering support in person, sometimes indirectly through training and supporting 'Listeners': prisoners selected and trained to undertake a Samaritan-type role for their fellow inmates. Use of the telephone allows another dimension here. In some cases prisoners simply make use of their allocated telephone time to make the call, but in other establishments a dedicated line is provided for this purpose. The importance of confidentiality in this context has required careful consultation and negotiation with the prison authorities in order to ensure that there is no conflict with their own duties and responsibilities, but they now accept this principle in relation to the content of all contacts between prisoners and Samaritans or Listeners.

Use of the technology for training, supervision and monitoring requires careful thought. In some counselling services contacts are recorded with the caller's permission for one or more of these purposes. The Samaritan position is that calls are not recorded in any circumstances. Whatever approach is taken, it is important that the caller is in some way made aware of the agency's policy. For a telephone service this is dictated by legal as well as ethical considerations. Discreet 'listening in' to calls, where, for instance, a second worker silently listens via an extra earpiece to the communication between caller and the person answering the call, is a rather fuzzier issue. This may be justified without the caller being explicitly made aware of it in individual cases, for example where the caller is in a very distressed state and the person answering the call needs guidance on how to proceed, or even to decipher what the caller is saying. It may also be justified in the early days of a new practitioner's experience, as part of their mentoring support. The guiding principle is that it should always be for the greater benefit of the caller.

If, for the sake of ensuring no dilution of the service to the individual caller, recording and unlimited listening in are both eschewed, monitoring of the service provision generally and the quality of individual workers' responses in particular, become thorny issues. Thorns or not, they must be grappled with by any agency which cares about the quality of its service. Samaritans has for many years operated a system of branch visits. Each branch is visited every three years by two experienced volunteers from other parts of the country who undertake, alongside the branch leadership, a thorough audit of its entire service. This practice has many strengths and plays a significant part in maintaining and improving quality and consistency, but no way has yet been found to include callers' views in the process.

Callers are undoubtedly the best judges of the effectiveness of the service, but a very distressed caller can hardly be asked to offer an evaluation before the call ends. If both confidentiality and anonymity are on offer, a statistically representative sampling at a later stage is almost impossible to achieve. Discussions with or questionnaires sent only to those who agree to participate, immediately bias the sample. It is generally acknowledged that this leaning will be in the direction of favourable responses since those who wish to cooperate in the venture are more likely to be 'satisfied customers'. It is in any case difficult to generate by this method a sample of sufficient size to justify the drawing of general conclusions.

There have been attempts to use more general market research as a 'piggy-back' mechanism for achieving a representative sample of views, for example work undertaken by Crossbow Research for Samaritans in 1999. The project inserted questions about Samaritans among questions relating to a variety of other topics, with the questionnaires being distributed to over 10,000 people selected to form a demographically representative cross-section of the general population. Responses were anonymous. Of these, 134 identified themselves as 'recent' callers. From their responses, Crossbow's report (unpublished, but made available internally throughout the organization in 2000) was able to draw useful conclusions in a number of areas. Some of these confirmed that the service was 'getting it right' in that particular respect, others indicated areas in which possible adjustments of emphasis were needed. The overall satisfaction ratings were reassuringly high. Although generally acknowledged to be a worthwhile exercise, not least because of its independence, the cost of such a venture is an inhibiting factor unless carried out as a goodwill gesture by a generous research company.

Market research might be one way forward in monitoring a service as a whole, but what of the issue of evaluating the individual performance of practitioners? It is well accepted that they should have mentors in the early stages of experience and supervision at all times. Is this enough, or do the dual roles of assisting the practitioner's skills development and assessing their performance sometimes conflict? One phrase that has crept into counselling literature from the world of commerce is that of 'mystery shopping', which in the present context would mean a programme of clandestine calls made by assessors posing as callers in need of the service. In this way, it is argued, workers are uninhibited by the knowledge of someone else listening to their responses and will proceed as they normally do. For this to be ethically acceptable it would have to be done only with the knowledge and full support of the whole workforce, otherwise mutual trust and teamwork would be irreparably damaged. But then the counterargument arises: if all are aware of the possibility that any call may be from a 'mystery shopper', would that not then colour their response to a genuine caller or at least prove a distraction from what should be their single-minded concentration on the caller's needs? There are many questions to be considered here, and no easy answers.

For organizations which rely largely on public donations for their existence and operation, questions of cost become a factor in some ethical equations. The question of whether to allow acceptance of reversed charge calls comes into this category, as does how to react to the vastly increased usage of mobile phones and the additional costs involved in these calls. Between the extreme positions of 'we do not accept reversed charge calls' and 'if the caller has requested this we should accept it and give them as much time as any other caller', lies a whole spectrum of possible stances. A balance of cost versus care needs to be struck. For example, it is possible to accept such calls and, while giving all necessary emotional support to the caller, to establish an early understanding that the additional cost should be borne in mind so as not to prolong the contact unnecessarily. Similarly, if the policy is to ring someone back if they request this and appear to need it, some qualification may be necessary if they are using a mobile phone.

In some telephone counselling services there will be in any case a mutually accepted timespan for each call, but in a service where the length of a call is normally matched to need on each occasion, judging how long should be allowed when other constraints come into play is far from straightforward. Quilliam tells a personal story which, while not in a counselling or purely emotional support setting, has in it a kernel of wisdom about balancing the needs of 'helper' and 'helped':

> Last summer, I was babysitting my godchild, Ellie. She's six. We usually have a mad time – you could say I'm never quite sure who's looking after who. But while chasing each other around the house, Ellie slipped and measured her length.
>
> No bones broken, no damage done. I got down to the serious business of cheering her up. Cold drink? No. Warm drink? No. Favourite video? No. Cuddle? No. I was at my wit's end. 'What do you need to feel better?' I demanded in the end, hands on hips.
>
> Ellie said, with all the gentle patience of a six year old explaining something to a grown-up, 'I'm not ready to feel better yet. What do *you* need to feel better?'
>
> (Quilliam 1999: 36)

Emergent issues

What of the future in work using counselling skills on the telephone? Ever-advancing telephone technology presents new ethical issues on an ongoing basis. It would now be technically possible to offer a service by text messaging. How effective could this be in terms of emotional support? If the instinct is to say not at all, perhaps we should think back to initial reactions some years ago to suggestions of offering such a service by email, now well proven. Keir (1986: 144) maintains that, 'One of the major shortcomings of our society is that we do not listen to each other. We *hear* what is being said to us but we are not *listening*.' Technology sometimes seems to exacerbate this, but it should assuredly be possible to embrace new developments which allow us to 'hear' the words, and find ways to add a caring listener: one who not only *receives* the words but gives attention to the implications of them, to the implications between them, and to what has been left unsaid.

An example of the use of a newly emergent technology was the development some years ago by Samaritans of a single national telephone number, or to be more precise, two numbers: one for the UK and one for the Republic of Ireland, a distinction dictated by the nature of the separate telephone systems. This enables equality of access for all who choose the telephone as their mode of contact, since calls are charged at the cost of a local call. Calls to this number 'hunt' through several Samaritan branches if necessary to find an unengaged line. The impact on reducing the engaged rate has been dramatic. But while this development has provided some answers to questions long asked of itself by the organization about equality of cost and availability of access, it has raised more questions in its wake, some as yet unanswered. For example, this 'single number' has in fact operated in parallel with the continued availability of local branch numbers. Callers to these numbers are now much more likely to get the engaged tone than callers on the single number. The logical extension might seem to be to discontinue local numbers and offer the service purely on the basis of the single number, but this then reduces the caller's choice of access should they wish to contact a particular branch. Where does the correct 'ethical point of balance' lie? This debate continues, and as technology advances so inevitably will others for any organization working on the telephone and determined to do so on a sound ethical basis.

References

BACP (2002) *Ethical Framework for Good Practice in Counselling and Psychotherapy*. Rugby: British Association for Counselling and Psychotherapy.

Bond, T. (1993) *Standards and Ethics for Counselling in Action*. London: Sage.

Eldrid, J. (1988) *Caring for the Suicidal*. London: Constable.

Keir, N. (1986) *I Can't Face Tomorrow*. Wellingborough: Thorsons.

Morgan, H.G. and Williams, R. (eds) (1994) *Suicide Prevention: The Challenge Confronted*, NHS Health Advisory Service Thematic Review. London: HMSO.

Quilliam, S. (1999) *What To Do When You Really Want To Help But Don't Know How*, 2nd edn. Brentwood: Transformation Press.

Rosenfield, M. (1997) *Counselling by Telephone*. London: Sage.

Samaritans (1981) *Seven Principles and Practices*, available from Samaritans General Office, The Upper Mill, Kingston Road, Ewell, Surrey KT17 2AF or on the website www.samaritans.org.uk

Sanders, P. (1993) *Using Counselling Skills on the Telephone*. Manchester: PCCS Books.

Shneidman, E.S. (1985) *Definition of Suicide*. New York: Wiley.

Telephone Helplines Association (1999) *Guidelines for Good Practice*, 3rd edn. London: Telephone Helplines Association.

4 Ethical thinking in online therapy

Kate Anthony and Stephen Goss

Types of modern communication technology develop quickly and change constantly, creating a need for consideration of not only how we can best conduct therapy using them but also whether we should be using them at all if ethical consideration cannot keep up with the progress. Debate over use of the Internet for global communication has mirrored discussion over the past twenty years or more regarding the use of the telephone for conducting a therapeutic relationship without a physical presence as a frame of reference (relying on the nuances of the spoken word alone). The most distinctive characteristic of Internet therapy is its use of only the written word to convey the core qualities needed to facilitate mental health, without any body language or audio cues at all.

This chapter explores some of the ethical implications of conducting therapy through the use of email and Internet relay chat (IRC), two of the most prolific uses of modern communications technology. All the ethical dimensions, issues and dilemmas are entirely subordinate to general ethical principles that can guide a practitioner in every situation. The principles of ethical behaviour are not changed – it is merely the details of their application that varies. Nonetheless, in Internet therapy there are considerations that are unusual in that the emergence of email and Internet chat as a means of conducting therapy in 1995 was client led. In much the same way as the Internet community itself developed, practitioners had to find an ethically acceptable way of working in the absence of guidelines, research or knowledge about how, or even if, Internet therapy could be considered to be beneficial. Suggested principles for conducting therapy over the Internet started to appear in the late

1990s from such organizations as the International Society for Mental Health Online (ISMHO) (1997), the National Board for Certified Counselors (NBCC) (1997, updated 2001), and the American Counseling Association (ACA) (1999). The British Association for Counselling and Psychotherapy (BACP) produced detailed guidelines (online and paper-based) for UK practitioners in 2001 (Goss *et al.* 2001), seeking international consultation to ensure as much knowledge of the method was used to inform their development as possible and that they would be widely applicable in the global context of the Internet.

Modern communication technology has a much further reach than just email and IRC, of course. Listservs (email to group facilities) have a large presence and can be utilized by supervisory groups, and the more public posting of messages on discussion boards on websites can have a useful function in Internet support and training groups. The development of broadband communication means that videoconferencing is becoming a more feasible method of conducting a face-to-face therapeutic relationship, not to mention developments in wireless telephone technology and stand-alone software programs for client use in the complete absence of the practitioner. In addition, there are specific issues that arise in relation to the Internet in society, such as the need for practitioners to appreciate the implications for clients whose use of the Internet includes 'cyberinfidelity', or escapism through use of Internet gaming or chatrooms (Anthony 2001). However, discussion of such topics remains mostly anecdotal at the time of writing; consequently, the rest of this chapter concentrates on forms of ethical thinking applicable to two, more researched modalities: email and IRC.

Characteristics of online therapy

A basic definition of email is that it is an asynchronous method of typed communication – that is, the parties do not need to be online at the same time to receive messages, and the content of messages may be written while offline and sent at a later date. This means that the content can be reconsidered and reworked many times over, impossible in a vocal conversation as in most traditional therapy. Delivery of email is usually very fast, but reading it can be delayed indefinitely, in contrast to, say, the telephone. Email does not have to be limited to one posting or delivery point like a postbox – it can be accessed and sent from any computer with Internet access anywhere in the world, and this flexibility of access is increasing as developments such as wireless mobile technology become more commonplace. Email can be printed off and stored electronically, inviting examination of a verbatim transcript of the therapy, much like making transcripts from audiotapes of sessions (but without the time cost involved in doing so). While printed copies of the therapy might be assumed to require treating in the same way as any records of therapy, electronic accounts are potentially more vulnerable given the relative ease with which they can be copied and circulated and the possibility of unauthorized access from a remote site. Here, the obvious additional ethical requirements are for practitioners to be aware of the risks, to take effective precautions and to ensure that clients are properly informed.

A basic definition of Internet relay chat (IRC) is that it is a synchronous method of typed communication – the parties involved have to be connected to the Internet and using compatible chatroom software to send messages back and forth in real time. The delay ('lag') between sending and receiving the message is usually less than a few seconds, creating a written dialogue similar to a face-to-face discussion but often, although not always, without any clues that the other party is preparing to speak. This means that limited experience of chatroom communication can be problematic when trying to create a flow of conversation. Like email, IRC sessions can be electronically stored and printed; but unlike email, there is only a limited amount of time during which the typed text can be reworked.

There are two central themes to these two text-based methods of communication via the Internet. The first theme consists of the *practical* characteristics that come with a means of delivering therapy that renders it available 24 hours a day, seven days a week and does so on a global scale, including the breakdown of barriers such as time, geography, access and organizational resources. The second theme consists of issues such as what psychological reasons there are for the client choosing to receive therapeutic help over the Internet rather than seeking face-to-face help. These could be overwhelming shame, the wish to remain anonymous, or difficulty with effectively communicating with speech owing to nervousness, anxiety or disability. Other characteristics include issues of practitioner competence and the increased possibilities for deception or deliberate presentation of an alternative persona (potentially by both practitioner and client).

Global communication

The ability to communicate globally is one of the most important features of email and IRC. With modern communications systems, this is now fast, simple and cheaper than letter-writing or making a telephone call, not to mention meeting face-to-face. This is so not only for international communication but also within countries where geography makes distance communication preferable to travelling, as in many rural areas as diverse as the Australian outback or the Highlands of Scotland. However, with vast distances between client and practitioner, emergency intervention becomes difficult in a crisis situation, particularly when asynchronous methods of communication are being used and the moment of crisis has been missed.

Issues of culture

The global function of Internet communication means that mental health services are now available to a much wider range of cultures, previously cut off by distance and remoteness. Furthermore, a member of a culture living outside their original geographical area can now be in direct contact with it via the Internet. With the ability to render physical distances irrelevant comes the possibility of having to cope with what may be vast cultural differences, creating a need for ethical consideration of their impact. For example, even very basic items such as what a potential client understands by the term 'counsellor', 'psychotherapist' or 'psychologist' may differ immensely, and practitioners have a corresponding duty to ensure that their services are clearly explained in advance. Cultural sensitivity is also more acutely necessitated by Internet therapy. Things that are readily familiar in, say, western cultures may be viewed quite differently elsewhere. For example, 'marriage guidance', familiar in some countries, has been reported to be expected to be concerned with increasing the ability of female clients to offer satisfaction in sexual and housekeeping matters (Al-Malki 2001). Working with those under the age of consent, and what that age is, carries very different implications in different parts of the world. The ability of a counsellor to be sensitive to the cultural experience of their client is a widely accepted feature of good quality therapy and practitioners may wish to question their ability to offer this to clients in countries far removed from their own.

Time zones

Global time zones are also redundant when using email to communicate, and are diminished when using IRC. Thus, a session that takes place for the client at 10am in the USA can be held at 5pm for the practitioner in the UK. Using email can mean that sessions take place at any time for either party, since the communication is asynchronous. However, along with these benefits comes the need for consideration of boundaries where access is available in different time zones and with 24-hour access. This is often an understated facet of online communication – clients can bombard their therapist with many emails and be distraught when as many replies are not forthcoming. These boundary issues have dictated a need for a new attitude towards thinking about practitioner availability and access, since usual consulting and office hours have been replaced with what is, potentially, 24-hour access. Experimentation with the benefits and disadvantages of being able to use consulting time differently has been (and still is) a learning curve for the profession.

Access

Another practical benefit of using computer-mediated communication is the ease of access for those somehow limited in accessing face-to-face facilities and who find it easier to use a home computer for mental health assistance. Examples of this are through physical disability, social anxiety or conditions such as agoraphobia. While the benefits to those who have different abilities seem obvious (both in use of adapted hardware and ease of access to the Internet rather than physical locations), ethical considerations of whether use of Internet therapy may exacerbate the latter conditions need to be addressed. The client whose social life takes place in virtual reality chatrooms may not benefit from another relationship, this time therapeutic, being offered and taking place in this way. Programmes that advocate full integration of online and offline life as being beneficial to mental health for individuals already exist (Suler 2002), but for those whose online life is excessive, a therapeutic online relationship may underline cyberspace as a more normal place to exist than in the physical world.

Critical situations and their ethical resolution

The characteristics of online communication described above have meant that the resolving of many of the ethical issues that they present has had to take place after their realization: it has not been possible to pre-empt them. Client demand for online therapeutic services meant that ethical thinking about their use has had to emerge from an attitude similar to that towards the Internet itself. From its earliest days, no one had any rules or guidelines for being in cyberspace. Indeed, one of its prime characteristics and most important attractions has been that it is an experimental environment the development of which is dependent on the people who avail themselves of it finding their own levels of use, perception and behaviour. The ethics of online therapy have developed from those practitioners who chose to use this form of communication in its earliest days, applying their own ethical stance in a new environment and finding a way of proceeding that seemed acceptable to them.

Competence

Before considering possible solutions to ethical dilemmas particular to the method, it is worth affirming the view of the authors that acceptable offline practitioner competence was and is the first consideration when considering transferring skills to the Internet. We do not see online work as suitable for the novice practitioner, and considerable experience is required before the transfer to this new environment can be made. Not least is the development of a sound ethical stance from which to build an online service. Furthermore, competence in a face-to-face environment should not be taken to imply competence in an online environment. There are additional areas of competence that are needed in cyberspace – over and above the obvious basics of adequate technological knowledge of hardware and software and an ability to use a keyboard quickly and efficiently. Cyberspace has its own norms and niceties about how people communicate, which developed out of the need to convey information as fast as possible since, for most people, typing is slower than speech

(Danet 2001: 17), and the subtleties of the psychology of Internet communication can be markedly different from using body language and tone of voice.

Suitability

There is still no firm opinion on who is or is not suitable for online therapy. Suicidal clients seem to be suitable for exclusion as their care is difficult from a distance, and yet work with this client group online can be successful (Barak 2001). Significant levels of personality disorder or schizophrenia are also seen by some to be a reason to exclude clients for this type of work, and yet email is already used by such clients for self-reporting symptoms and feelings, allowing practitioners to intercept breakdowns (Childress and Williams 2002). Stofle (2001) provides a 'level of care' table giving an idea of appropriate mental stability when considering an online relationship for therapy, including suicidal/homicidal tendencies, ability to form relationships, participation in the world, reality testing and emotional management. It is the responsibility of the practitioner to ensure that they have robust procedures in place, particularly at the assessment stage, to identify clients who are unlikely to benefit from, or indeed who could be damaged by, a course of online therapy.

Another important ethical issue is practitioner competence, regardless of the means by which therapy is delivered. It should be assumed, perhaps, that client groups with whom a practitioner is not competent to work offline are also ones that they are not competent to work with online. Gaining an awareness of the client's experience of cyberspace is advisable, such as whether they spend vast amounts of time in virtual reality sites, or habitually or obsessively form idealized relationships with people they meet online. An Internet-enabled pathology (King 2000) may not be helped by a therapeutic relationship conducted online.

Contracting: crisis intervention, cultural consideration and process

Clarity of contracting is one of the most important aspects of working online because of the complexities of the issues involved and the relative lack of awareness many Internet users have of them, such as the limitations on privacy. It should not be assumed that when a client ticks a box stating they have read and understood information regarding the process and contract that they actually have done so: the website contract should be restated in the body of an email as a double-check. The client must be able to make an informed decision on whether to proceed – the practitioner's responsibility is to put them in a position to do so and verify that this has been done. Different contexts will demand different contracts, but supplying detailed information on the possible limitations of the service and the lack of research on its efficacy is, perhaps, the most ethically secure position a practitioner can take when forming a service.

Crisis intervention is difficult online, especially when a client is using a free Internet-based email system, where the account can be closed quickly and registration information can be faked. There is little a practitioner can do if an email client is at risk of harming either themself or others and then closes their email account if steps have not been taken at the pre-therapy stage for back-up emergency systems, such as a telephone number. However, many practitioners would also see this as defeating the object of being able to offer a safe, anonymous service. Use of a telephone, even in such extreme circumstances, has implications about privacy and confidentiality – if family members discover the existence of the relationship, for example. These are all issues that the client needs to be aware of in the contracting stage in order to make an informed decision about continuing. A second way in which the practitioner can behave responsibly is to take it upon themself to learn the cultural context of healthcare in a crisis in the region where the client lives, and also what local face-to-face resources might be available if an emergency situation arose.

The responsibility for learning about a client's cultural context reaches beyond crisis intervention in that an awareness of the sensitivity needed to conduct a therapeutic relationship across cultures is paramount if the practitioner is to behave ethically. This awareness has implications for deciding whether the cultural barriers should be crossed at all, or whether the client should be found resources with a greater depth of understanding of their cultural norms. Information in this context is easily accessed on the Internet, although it can be notoriously unreliable. Thorough research about a client's culture may be required to enable the therapist to make an informed decision about whether they feel comfortable crossing cultural boundaries.

Clear indications of how the therapy process will work should also be provided for the client, including length of emails, when the client may expect a response, and the length of an IRC session. It is possible to send an email automatically, similar to those used in business as an 'out-of-office auto-reply', which can inform a client when to expect a reply and what to do if they are in crisis, such as providing a contact number for the therapist or local information about resources. How the client will be charged, if appropriate, must also be conveyed, along with provision of secure transaction facilities as standard. Firm boundaries must be put in place and adhered to as to how available the practitioner is to the client when Internet access allows emails to be sent indiscriminately and many Internet service providers (ISPs) have functions that allow clients to know when a therapist is online for whatever reason. Correct use and knowledge of the facilities to block such functions should be handled with care. For instance, good practice may be seen as blocking other people from knowing you are online automatically when logging on and only then allowing them access to you when appropriate, rather than their seeing your arrival in cyberspace and knowing they have been blocked if they try to contact you, which can be hurtful to a vulnerable client. This sort of issue is a good example of one of the newer ethical dilemmas that have had to be addressed in retrospect as software sophistication increases to allow such functions.

A further practical concern for practitioners using the Internet is reliance on the hardware and software systems themselves and the vagaries of the Internet. ISPs can close down or withdraw services or may prove to be incompatible with other ISPs; destructive files such as viruses can disrupt software; hardware becomes out of date and unable to handle rapidly developing technology; and computers crash for no discernible reason. Working with technology that gets disrupted (or simply will not work) is at best a frustration and at worst risks psychologically damaging effects on the vulnerable client who is reliant on these methods of communication for their mental well-being.

Confidentiality and anonymity

Common to all these benefits is the ongoing discussion about levels of confidentiality and data protection that can be offered when using the Internet. This includes not only the points at which emails may be intercepted as they travel through cyberspace, but also the possibility of a third party gaining access to material held on either the practitioner's or the client's computer. Examples include the case of an abusive spouse having particular interest in the content of the sessions, and ISPs or technical support staff viewing emails in order to check for viruses or illegal content.

Also particular to this way of working is the ease with which mistakes can happen in sending the message itself – many email programs self-complete email addresses from address books, and sending confidential material to the wrong party is easily done. Organizations that use internal facilities (intranets) for therapeutic assistance face further confidentiality issues. Resources for employee or student mental healthcare are often scarce and the use of electronic communication is increasingly seen as a potential answer in providing a therapeutic service to employees or students in an efficient manner. However, decisions on which members of the organization have access to sensitive material held on corporate servers have to be made. Confidentiality of client material may also be compromised if practitioners use electronic means to discuss casework in a supervisory relationship without careful safeguards. There are also ethical implications on confidentiality if a client's access to the Internet relies on a public computer such as in a cybercafé or library, in that the emails may be accessible to the next user or that IRC sessions can be watched.

There are several ways of ensuring that confidentiality of client material is maintained when using modern communications technology, and knowledge of their use, and their limitations, carries particular ethical implications for work in this field. Encryption software is often free and can provide secure scrambled messages that only the practitioner and client can unlock. Data protection issues can be treated as for face-to-face work for paper-based storage of sessions or notes, but electronic forms of databasing will need further consideration regarding who can access them and how. Use of password protection of these files is always advisable but additional measures may be required. The ability to hack into client sessions can be made less attractive by the use of member access only areas on some websites. The practitioner has a duty to maintain their hardware and software systems to the optimum level, limiting as far as possible the event of system failure. Damage to their own and client computers can also be avoided by installing – and regularly updating – virus protection software and strong firewalls. A willingness to download and upgrade compatible communications software is required, putting the client's preferred method of communication before the practitioner's. In addition, information on what will happen in the event of technical breakdown, although more pertinent to IRC than to email, could be arranged with the client through the use of a telephone call where appropriate.

The ability to be anonymous to your therapist, or to create a different identity, can sometimes be unproblematic and may even provide a useful function for the client in acting out different parts of their psyche, but it can also be seen as an expression of pathology and is of particular concern when assessing a client's state of mind. Clients may also present a 'false' image of themselves in face-to-face therapy as well, of course, and in most respects there is little difference in online work except that relatively gross deceptions are more readily achieved, such as switching of sex. If such deliberate manipulation of one's apparent character is revealed or otherwise discovered, the therapist might themself feel abused, of course, but is faced with the possibility of tapping a rich seam of therapeutic material and in either case can proceed just as they would do in any other setting. Just as in face-to-face therapy, were a therapist to indulge in deception of clients, the ethical issues would be quite different and the practitioner would almost always be considered entirely in the wrong (Van Gelder 1996).

Anonymity also holds problems in the case of minors communicating on the Internet without parental permission and there is no guarantee that use of a credit card indicates that the client is over 18. Safety of the client is difficult to manage in these situations, although it is undoubtedly possible as the work of the Samaritans in the UK with people at risk of suicide testifies (Lago *et al.* 1999).

Disinhibition

Another feature of online communication is what Suler (1997) has termed the 'disinhibition effect'. This is the tendency for online communicators to be much more open, honest and frank than they would be in a face-to-face meeting and to become so rather more quickly. This suggests (Anthony 2000) that there is opportunity for the therapeutic relationship to develop more rapidly, but there is also the danger of clients being able access thoughts usually contained through various defences and becoming overwhelmed by their emotions and discoveries about themselves. Even when such openness is experienced as beneficial, and writing very long and intense emails can undoubtedly be cathartic for some clients, care of the practitioner must also be considered as must their response. Receiving large amounts of concentrated, emotionally distressing material – asynchronously and before the therapeutic relationship has been established – can be stressful, not to mention highly time consuming, and also requires great skill in responding appropriately, thoroughly and sensitively to all the important strands that are raised.

Practitioners should consider the openness facilitated by Internet communication as a potential benefit but they have an ethical responsibility to ensure that the client is not overwhelmed by the amount of emotion they experience and that they protect themselves from being overwhelmed by being able to keep the emails focused on what is achievable within the contract length. This is a skill that comes with training and experience and therapists will form their own style in being able to guide the client in what is appropriate. This openness also means that a therapeutic relationship can develop quickly, forcing the creation of a fantasy of the practitioner that can often be idealized. This should be recognised by the therapist and measures taken, carefully, in conveying to the client that their presence and availability in cyberspace is not unlimited, and that the interpretation of the text is the client's, and may have been quite different if it had been conveyed verbally and with interpretation of body language being possible.

Fantasy

Fantasy of the therapist (and client) is another area of Internet-delivered therapy that warrants further research. Where physical clues as to how the other person looks or sounds are withheld, a visual and auditory fantasy is inevitably developed that may be far from the reality. Space prevents a full examination of this interesting theoretical characteristic of online communication here, but the issue has ethical implications for those practitioners who intend to use face-to-face sessions later in the relationship.

Building an ideal therapist in the imagination may provide a useful function for the client in helping their recovery but, conversely, meeting the reality of the therapist can shatter illusions built and maintained to the detriment of the client's well-being. Brice (2000) cites a case in transferring from email to a physical relationship where the client, being used to the rational articulation that email affords, expected the practitioner to talk in much the same way as she imagined his voice when reading the emails. In addition, it is widely recognized that the Internet tends to level the balance of power between two communicators; this tendency may be translated to the therapeutic relationship in that the client holds more nearly equal power than in the face-to-face relationship where the practitioner usually has control of the environment.

Internet 'addiction'

There is no evidence that online therapy exacerbates Internet-enabled pathologies, or what has also been called an Internet addiction disorder (Young 1996). However, detailed knowledge of some of the social and relationship problems that can occur if a client is spending large amounts of time in cyberspace is needed if the therapist is to achieve empathy with a client's situation. There is a range of issues related to Internet usage. For example, an understanding is needed of the emotional ramifications of behaviour it may seem impossible to achieve online, such as a virtual rape taking place in a chatroom (Dibbell 1993). Use of the Internet for a client may also include their own weblog ('blog' – a personal webpage which usually takes the form of a journal) or discussion boards which could include details of the therapy, and the therapist, in a public forum. Ownership of therapeutic material and controls on its use are important elements in the power balance between therapist and client, and discussion of the appropriate use of the transcripts with the client should be included in contracting. It is also possible to follow the client undetected through cyberspace outside of the sessions, for example to track their behaviour patterns if they are an avid user of Internet facilities. In general, of course, if this were done without the client's consent it would be considered unethical behaviour on the part of the practitioner.

Supervision, training and regulation

Supervision is currently an area of debate in online mental health communities. It is arguable that the online therapist should have an online supervisor who has considerable online experience. However, these supervisors are few and far between and most online practitioners rely on peer supervision, such as the work of the ISMHO

Clinical Case Study Group (see Fenichel *et al.* 2002). Just as online therapy was (and some would say still is) an experimental process when it first emerged, such is online supervision currently. Practitioners who embark on online therapy must find a suitable level of supervision for client work while the platform develops if they are to work within ethical boundaries.

An ethical stance on the importance of continuing professional development has led to the emergence of training courses that encompass basic online communication, ethical considerations of the modality as outlined here and the emerging theoretical and practical knowledge available thus far. Such courses should be undertaken by any therapist wishing to make the transfer to online work now that they are available and are based on the experience of online therapists who pioneered working in this way. It is no longer good enough to state that this is a new field and no one has answers to how it should be done. Recognition is also needed that research posted on the Internet does not guarantee any level of quality – practitioners need to be able to make an informed decision as to whether research, anecdotal or otherwise, is of value in informing their ethical and theoretical stance in relation to such work. Professional associations, like the BACP, already provide mechanisms for redress in the event of, say, a client wanting to complain about the behaviour of their therapist or the quality of their care. Few, if any, however, have mechanisms put up specifically to deal with online provision. It is debatable whether such specialist regulatory mechanisms would be needed or whether the ethical safeguards that underlie all counselling and psychotherapy would be sufficient.

Emergent issues

The new field of counselling and psychotherapy carried out over the Internet still has a long way to go. Further ethical issues will undoubtedly be uncovered as the practice becomes increasingly attractive in an increasing number of situations. The absence of definitive outcome research on its efficacy relative to, say, traditional face-to-face methods might be thought to suggest that it is as yet premature for practitioners to be offering such services at all. However, the evidence base is steadily developing and the largely anecdotal evidence available is encouraging, suggesting that the evident demands for Internet therapy services from clients are not made without good reason. Issues such as the regulation of services, not least in a global health service economy, are yet to be effectively addressed although an increasing number of professional associations, including the BACP, are introducing rules and guidance for their members in individual countries around the world. Whether there would be advantages in a global professional association of online therapists that has real regulatory power, and whether such a thing would be achievable given the vast disparity in the legal and professional structures in different parts of the world, are yet to be seen. Some groups, such as the International Society for Mental Health Online, are taking steps by facilitating the essential dialogue between practitioners but quality control and the ethical safeguard of effective complaints procedures remain elusive.

Future developments in communications technology seem likely to continue to outstrip the development of definitive information on, or guidance pertinent to, their use. It is not possible in a brief chapter to consider all the possible emerging technologies but it seems likely that developments such as the use of avatars (computer-generated representations of physical presence), natural language engines (software that is programmed to recognize human communication and respond in a like manner), haptic body suits (allowing tactile experience of virtual spaces), videoconferencing, stand-alone software and virtual reality will all present new challenges, not least those of ensuring that an adequate evidence base is provided for their use and that guidance on their use is made available. It is already possible for both client and therapist to conduct therapy in more or less any location thanks to mobile telecommunications and the availability of ever more portable computers, and such things are already well established. The need for attention to detail by practitioners in ensuring that their working environment is suitable and that clients are aware of the threat to confidentiality when, for example, using a computer in a public place, underscores the general theme in online working of commonplace ethical issues being given an added urgency as normal working practices are adapted to the technological world.

Early identification of safe and ethical practices will remain perhaps the most important consideration for all those, clients and practitioners alike, with an interest in the field. Indeed, an exciting feature of the Internet is precisely that it provides a means for a high level of social and intellectual freedom. Any profession that is not slowly to ossify into irrelevance must be open and adaptable to innovative ways of working and must deal with both their positive and negative possibilities.

References

Al-Malki, M. (2001) Attitudes to family and marriage counselling in Qatar. Paper presented to the Scottish Counselling Research Conference, University of Abertay Dundee, Dundee, November.

American Counseling Association (1999) *Ethical Standards for Internet On-Line Counseling*, available at http://www.counseling.org/resources/internet.htm (accessed 5 December 2002).

Anthony, K. (2000) Counselling in cyberspace, *Counselling Journal*, 11(10): 625–7. Also available at www.kateanthony.co.uk (accessed 5 December 2002).

Anthony, K. (2001) Online relationships and cyberinfidelity, *Counselling Journal*, 12(9): 38–9. Also available at www.kateanthony.co.uk (accessed 5 December 2002).

Barak, A. (2001) SAHAR: An Internet-based emotional support service for suicidal people. Paper presented at a conference of the British Psychological Society, Psychology and the Internet: A European Perspective, Farnborough, November. Available at http://construct.haifa.ac.il/~azy/sahar02.htm (accessed 5 December 2002).

Brice, A. (2000) Therapeutic support using e-mail: a case study, *Counselling*, 12(2): 100–1.

Childress, C. and Williams, J. (2002) Incorporating email into patient care at community mental health clinics. Paper presented at the 110th American Psychological Association Convention, Chicago, August.

Danet, B. (2001) *Cyberplay*. Oxford: Berg.

Dibbell, J. (1993) A rape in cyberspace, *The Village Voice*, 21 December: 36–42. Available at www.apocalypse.org/pub/u/lpb/muddex/vv.html (accessed 6 June 2002).

Fenichel, M., Suler, J., Barak, A. *et al.* (2002) Myths and realities of online clinical work. Available at www.fenichel.com/myths (accessed 2 July 2002).

Goss, S.P., Anthony, K., Palmer, S. and Jamieson, A. (2001) *BACP Guidelines for Online Counselling and Psychotherapy*. Rugby: British Association for Counselling and Psychotherapy.

International Society for Mental Health Online (1997) *Suggested Principles for the Online Provision of Mental Health Services*. Current update (2002) at http://www.ismho.org/suggestions.html (accessed 5 December 2002).

King, S.A. (2000) Internet enabled pathology: is the Internet addictive, or are addicts using the Internet? Paper presented at Internet Research 1.0: The State of the Interdiscipline, the first annual convention of the Association of Internet Researchers, University of Kansas, Lawrence, Kansas, September.

Lago, C., Baughan, R., Copinger-Binns, P. *et al.* (1999) *Counselling Online . . . Opportunities and Risks in Counselling Clients via the Internet*. Rugby: British Association for Counselling and Psychotherapy.

National Board for Certified Counselors (NBCC) (1997) *Standards for the Ethical Practice of WebCounseling*. Current update (1991) *The Practice of Internet Counseling*. Available at http://www.nbcc.org/ethics/webethics.htm (accessed 5 December 2002).

Stofle, G. (2001) *Choosing an Online Therapist*. Harrisburg, PA: White Hat Communications.

Suler, J. (1997) *The Online Disinhibition Effect: The Psychology of Cyberspace*. Available at http://www.rider.edu/users/suler/psycyber/disinhibit.html (accessed 5 December 2002).

Suler, J. (2002) *Equest: A Comprehensive Online Program for Self-study and Personal Growth*. Available at http://www.rider.edu/users/suler/psycyber/equest.html (accessed 5 December 2002).

Van Gelder, L. (1996) The strange case of the electronic lover, in R. Kling (ed.) *Computerisation and Controversy*. London: Academic Press.

Young, K. (1996) Pathological Internet use: the emergence of a new clinical disorder. Presentation at University of Pittsburgh at Bradford, August, *APA Monitor*, American Psychological Association. Available at http://www.apa.org/releases/internet.html

5 Ethical thinking in couple counselling and therapy

Derek Hill

The characteristics of, and practitioner training for, couple therapy

Couple therapy[1] is an enterprise that is subject to pressures analogous to those affecting couple relationships themselves. The needs of the partners as individuals, of children and kinfolk, and of the larger community, all press for attention. The couple relationship being the client, the therapist's task is to manage the tension between competing voices, focusing on others only to the extent that is necessary to assist the partners to evaluate, and perhaps seek to change, influences that affect their capacity to make choices about the nature of their relationship.

In England and Wales, therapeutic work with couples was the earliest manifestation of initiatives that have resulted in a wide variety of forms of counselling and psychotherapy being available to the general public today. It remains largely the province of the voluntary agencies which were responsible for introducing and developing it over the past 60 or more years (Lewis *et al.* 1992). Today, services are offered to those in common law relationships and in lesbian or gay relationships, as well as to married couples and those forming or ending relationships. Work with second and subsequent relationships, and the problems arising in 'blended' families, are a growing part of couple therapists' work. Some couple therapists also offer psychosexual therapy and others staff schemes specifically designed to address domestic violence. Educational programmes preparing people for adult relationships and for parenting have been provided by the 'marital' agencies since their earliest days, often using the skills and insights of couple therapists in their design and delivery.

Couple therapy is available in a variety of forms. Brief, solution-focused couple therapy may involve no more than a single session. Much of the work undertaken by the voluntary agencies is accomplished in about six sessions. More extended work lasting a year or more and based on weekly sessions is provided by some practitioners and is able to address some more intractable relationship problems, the needs of couples coping with mental health issues or a partner's serious illness, or the needs of couples engaged in major life transitions (Carter and McGoldrick 1989). Many couple therapists are willing to work with only one partner, although most casework is conducted with both partners present. The theoretical approaches employed are diverse, as is illustrated by contemporary texts on couple therapy (Jacobson and Margolin 1979; Freeman 1982; Willi 1982, 1984; Gurman 1985; Bornstein and Bornstein 1986; James and Wilson 1986; Chasin *et al.* 1990; Scharff and Scharff 1991; Bockus, 1993; Bubenzer and West 1993; Johnson and Greenberg 1994; Weeks and Hof 1994; Crane 1996; Gilbert and Schmukler 1996; Jacobson and Christensen 1996; Rabin 1996; Butler and Joyce 1998; Brown 1999).

While the earliest forms of training in couple work were designed for laypersons with no previous experience of the role of counsellor (Lewis *et al.* 1992), today's training programmes are increasingly designed for those with some experience of casework. Though no longer limited to the offerings of the major 'marital' agencies (Relate, Marriage Care, Couple Counselling Scotland, Tavistock Marital Studies Institute), such training programmes are many fewer in number than those devoted to the preparation of the various kinds of individual therapist. However, courses currently range from 20-week part-time introductions to marital and couple therapy (London Marriage Guidance) to three-year part-time postgraduate studies leading to masters degrees (Relate). The preponderant theoretical model in the UK is psychodynamic although some agencies have evolved programmes leading to the development of couples practice with an integrative approach (Relate). There has been a notable convergence in the theoretical underpinnings of couple therapy and family therapy, something that has enriched the casework and the professional development programmes of both kinds of practitioner.

Hooper (1985) contrasts the relative abundance of research papers on couple therapy in the USA with the dearth of empirical studies in Britain. Crowe (1978) and Bennun (1984) each carried out controlled comparisons of different forms of couple work. More recently McCarthy *et al.* (1998) carried out a study involving 2073 clients of Relate in the Midlands and Northern Ireland which assessed responses to couple counselling. Among many findings, one is of particular relevance to this book. The researchers wrote:

> Our research produced evidence that men and women tend to want different things out of counselling. In particular, women seem more concerned than men about personal feelings. Men tend to focus on solving problems rather than gaining self-understanding, and seem less concerned about being understood by counsellors. If couples diverge with regard to expectations it becomes difficult for counsellors to satisfy both partners.
>
> (McCarthy *et al.* 1998: 100)

The dilemma faced by couple counsellors as a result of this difference is discussed in the next section.

This author was introduced to couple therapy by the training offered by the National Marriage Guidance Council (NMGC, now Relate) in the early 1970s. Rogers' approach (1942, 1973), the findings of Truax and Carkhuff (1967), the early writings of Egan (1975) and NMGC's own authors (Hooper and Roberts 1967; Venables 1971; Mace 1972; Guiver 1973;) all had their impact, but the source most often returned to during the intervening quarter of a century is Henry Dicks' *Marital Tensions* (1967). In that period I benefited from training, lectures, consultations and literature provided by the Tavistock Marital Studies Institute and informed by a psychoanalytic approach (Pincus 1960; Bannister and Pincus 1965; Guthrie and Mattinson 1971; Mattinson 1975; Pincus and Dare 1978; Clulow 1985; Ruszczynski 1993; Fisher 1999). Latterly, postmodernism and social constructionist thinking has introduced an 'and' into the theoretical underpinnings of casework which has been enriching, most of all for clients not constrained by an allegiance to one model of human experience. The author now wears the label 'integrative' and warms to the writings of McNamee and Gergen (1992), Flaskas and Perlesz (1996) and Flaskas (2002), as well as Fonagy (2001) and Clulow (2001).

Critical situations and their ethical resolution

The fundamental dilemma

As has already been stated, it is the couple relationship that is the couple therapist's client. That relationship is primarily the construct of the adult partners who together embody it. The characteristics of the relationship, itself unique, are revealed during therapy through the interactions of the couple and the therapist. Typically, three distinct sources of information and insights into the relationship are available to the therapist:

- Partner A's experience of and responses to the relationship and the therapist, as well as the therapist's own reactions to that 'story'.
- Partner B's experience of and responses to the relationship and the therapist, as well as the therapist's own reactions to that 'story'.
- The couple's joint responses to the circumstances in which they find themselves, including the therapy, and the therapist's own responses to being engaged in that 'drama'.

It will be apparent that these three primary sources may reinforce each other and together provide a coherent description of the relationship, the values and attitudes that inform it, the roles occupied by the partners within it, its emotional resources, and its adaptability to changing life situations, as well as illustrating the partners' characteristic interactions. A capacity to accommodate, *to celebrate*, differences is a source of richness and strength in couple relationships, and that capacity may be evident to the therapist as the couple describe and enact their relationship in therapy sessions. On the other hand, those sources may be dissonant, may evidence lacunae, and may suggest the causes of deep-seated, unresolved and disabling conflicts.

Embedded in those bodies of information are invitations to collude (with one or other partner, family members, or society at large), to favour familiar value systems and cultural norms rather than grapple with the unfamiliar, and to give credibility to powerfully and clearly presented perceptions and thus discount less well comprehended perspectives. The couple therapist is constantly challenged by two questions: 'What meanings attach to the words and acts presented?' and 'What is it, among all that has been presented, that is central to work focused on the future of the couple relationship?' The reality is that the therapist is not in a position to provide reliable answers to either question. It is the couple who are 'experts on their own relationship' yet who may also have separate and shared reasons for being unhelpful about using their expertise for the purposes of therapy. Here lies the root of the couple therapist's fundamental ethical dilemma.

> Ruth and John were attending their second session with their therapist. From the first session it had been evident that Ruth had initiated the couple's entry into therapy. She had had a lot to say and several of her reflections on the nature and state of her relationship with John had intrigued the therapist because she had alluded to both John's and her own patterns of defensive behaviour. John had limited himself to saying that he thought their relationship was 'basically OK' and had volunteered no information or opinions. He had sat, watchful but silent, thoughout that session. In efforts to secure John's positive engagement in the work the therapist had opened the second session by inviting both partners, one at a time, John first, to comment on their experiences during the first session. John's contribution was to the effect that it was unclear to him and, he guessed, to the therapist why the two of them had come seeking help. He said that they were in a sound financial situation, their house was pleasant, they each had their own interests and friends, and they didn't argue when they were together. Ruth then spoke, more in sadness than anger, she said that everything that John had said was factually correct but that none of it had anything to do with the fact that their relationship was an empty shell in spite of her best efforts to inject some energy and emotion into it. As the second session progressed, the contrast between the perspectives of the partners became more extreme.[2]

In this vignette, the therapist heard two very different stories and was aware of feeling rather censorious towards John though sad for, and in sympathy with, Ruth. Reflection on the relationship being presented drew attention to a sense of unvoiced tensions and angriness, a lack of emotional connection between the partners, and to the therapist's inclination to engage with great caution with a relationship that was like a bomb about to explode. The couple's purposes in seeking therapy had not been made explicit and it might be questioned whether shared purposes existed.

To the point described above, the therapist's objective was the fostering of a purposive therapeutic alliance with the couple seen as partners in a relationship. That objective was adopted because the therapeutic relationship is perceived to be pivotal by theorists affiliated to several of the most prominent approaches to therapy (Rogers 1957; Casement 1985; Flaskas and Perlez 1996), because research studies show that the quality of that relationship is a primary indicator of the effectiveness of casework (Clarkson 1995), and because continuing attention given to the state of the therapeutic alliance is an essential part of the process by which ethical casework is sustained. It might be argued that therapists who are committed to the development of therapeutic relationships by exercising genuineness, congruence, unconditional positive regard, acceptance, and empathic understanding (Rogers' core conditions – see Mearns and Thorne 1988) are actively giving expression to all the values and principles at the heart of the BACP's *Ethical Framework* (2002).

It is helpful to consider the couple therapist's initial engagement with the partners in terms of a duty of care, itself a legal concept as well as an expression of a responsibility to conduct therapy in an ethical fashion. A duty of care for the couple relationship is self-evident, but the therapist also has a duty of care for the partners as individuals. Since those individuals may have different needs and expectations the therapist is obliged to act in an even-handed manner when engaging with them. The partners in a conflicted relationship are likely to experience powerful anxieties about self-disclosure in the presence of one another, so much so that the need to protect the self may initially outweigh any motivation to focus on their relationship's well-being. Figure 5.1 illustrates the situation and the manoeuvre that the therapist must undertake.

By giving attention to, and establishing the core conditions with, each partner separately in an even-handed manner, the therapist works to demonstrate to both partners that, as individuals, they are being offered a containing environment in which their thoughts and feelings will be heard, respected and valued. Progressively, as the individuals' concerns to protect themselves reduce, the therapist

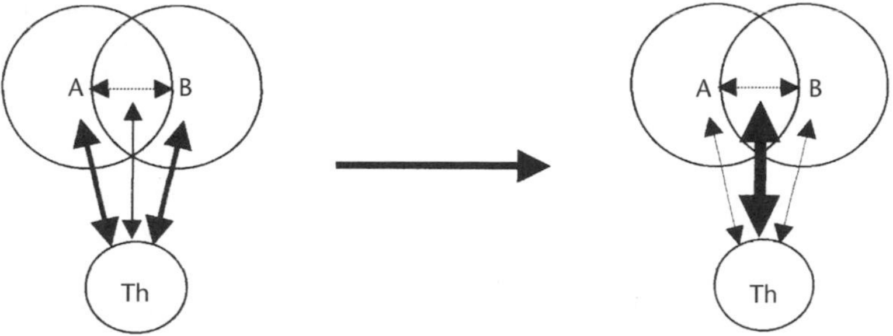

Figure 5.1 Therapist (Th) working to establish core conditions with the partners and for the couple relationship

addresses both in terms of their relationship with one another, building a focus for the work which is predominantly on the relationship. That is to say, an opportunity to focus attention on the couple relationship is created for the partners by ensuring that each, individually, has a trusted working relationship with the therapist.

Throughout the process described the therapist holds in mind:

- that the couple relationship is the client;
- that the couple are the experts on their relationship;
- the need to identify the meaning(s) (for the partners) of the words and acts presented;
- the need to identify the issues that are central (for the partners) to work focused on the future nature of the relationship.

Together these working assumptions and needs require of the therapist a capacity to sustain a state of 'not knowing' in order to engage with the client's world as fully as possible. As this iterative process takes place there is a distinction to be made between the ethical responsibilities of therapists who use only one theoretical approach and those whose approach is eclectic/integrative. The former have the task of working towards a determination of whether the couple's individual and shared resources and their world-view(s) make their situation amenable to being 'storied' in an understandable way in language congruent with the therapist's theoretical approach, or whether a referral to a more appropriate source of therapeutic assistance is necessary. The latter have a responsibility to avoid the premature adoption of a particular theoretical perspective and the associated hypothesis-building since that 'knowing' can distort the process of learning about the client's realities. They must also keep in mind the possibility that referral of the couple may be the most appropriate option.

> Ethical issues arose during the first moments of contact between the therapist, John and Ruth. The couple very quickly provided information which suggested that the partners had different styles, world-views and personal resources. They also prompted quite powerful emotional responses in the therapist, as did their troubled relationship.

The therapist's internal disciplines and recursive processing of events within the therapy ('reflexivity' – see Burnham 1986) assisted an understanding of the use being made of self for the benefit of the partners, and the uses the partners were making of the therapist. That processing also permitted the monitoring of the 'even-handedness' with which the partners were being engaged in the therapy. This attention given to the detail of the therapy's early transactions equips the therapist with information and brings to awareness influences which must be taken into account when key decisions are made about the form, content and duration of therapy – *the couple therapist's fundamental dilemma*.

A couple relationship is the shared possession of the partners, and the couple therapist is obliged from an ethical standpoint to work to shape a therapeutic process which enables both of the partners to engage fully in it, and thereby use all their personal resources to serve its purposes. Technically, this demands the synthesis of a lexicon and adoption of patterns of transactions which reflect, utilize and augment the couple's unique combination of insights, awarenesses, experiences, knowledge and skills. It is not a task that can be undertaken by the therapist alone. It is a matter of negotiation and one in which the therapist's 'not knowing' should assist by disposing both the partners to contribute from their own perspectives. As it proceeds, the therapist's particular role is that of articulating shared understandings and agreements. In so doing the therapist assembles the material to be woven into one or more hypotheses about the nature of the couple relationship and its needs. When the therapist is able to offer to the partners purposes for the therapy which they recognize and can own, and when their relationship can be described to them in language which makes sense to them both, and is also a verbalization of the therapist's working hypotheses based on one or more selected theoretical approaches, that negotiation process is nearing completion of its first cycle.

> During their third session with the therapist, John and Ruth acknowledged how very differently they thought about their relationship and they began to wonder to what extent there was common ground between them in terms of what they wanted from their life together. Both said they wanted the relationship to continue and to improve. Neither thought that influences external to themselves limited their options in important ways. Each asked the therapist to help them to find ways to make their relationship more enjoyable, rewarding and important.

John and Ruth provided a challenging example of the kinds of differences between partners which McCarthy *et al.* (1998) identified in the passage from their report quoted earlier. If seen separately for individual therapy, John and Ruth might have been offered quite different forms of therapy. Ruth's insights into the less obvious characteristics of her patterns of relating could have led to work based on a psychodynamic formulation of the issues she faced. John's concern to identify and solve problems might have resulted in a commitment to solution-focused therapy. Seen as a couple, their joint request for work to improve their relationship gave a particular significance to the ethics-based idea of even-handedness. Not only must the partners be offered therapy dedicated to the enrichment of their relationship, but that therapy must be offered in a form and using a language that actively assists them both to make their unique contribution to the task. Those are simple ideas but they call heavily on the resilience of the therapeutic alliance with each of the partners individually, and with them jointly as a couple. They make demands on the therapist's capacity to understand and take account of the influences that might lead to the subtle skewing of the work in ways that favoured one or other partner through collusions or the unwarranted influence of the therapist's own values and priorities. Not least, they call on the creativity of all the three persons in the consulting room. When successfully negotiated, this phase of couple counselling is a telling illustration of the central role of ethical considerations and their ability to serve as the catalyst for the creative use of hypothesizing, therapeutic strategies and interventions.

Casework of this kind disposes the therapist to regard ethical dilemmas as opportunities to engage with clients creatively rather than seeing them as problems which require a defensive response and which constrain the work. Although its starting point is in deontological ethics (the duty of care), its creativity springs from a teleological stance (ends valued above actions). That movement between forms of ethical thinking defines the casework described as being based on a pluralist approach to ethics.

Kinds of critical situation

Couple casework throws up a very wide variety of situations that present the therapist with an ethical dilemma, and it is helpful to place those situations into one of two broad categories that derive from the notion that couple relationships have both public and private domains (Clark and Haldane 1990). The public domain has to do with the couple's relationship with society – marriage contracts, divorce, parental responsibilities, criminal activities and so on. Situations that raise public domain issues thus demand attention to the dictates of the legal system as well as to the imperatives of ethical practice. The impact of social norms and the prevailing legal system is less clear-cut when considering issues in the private domain – the couple's intimate shared life. The latter category of critical situations is that in which ethical considerations typically predominate, though it should be noted that some issues have migrated from private to public domains, for example, rape in marriage and domestic violence. A situation located in each of those two domains is discussed here. It will be seen that those situations present the therapist with what may be regarded as variants of the fundamental dilemma.

The privacy and confidentiality of therapy

The privacy of couple therapy depends on commitments made by both the clients and the therapist. It is negotiated to help ensure that material disclosed by the clients for the purposes of the therapy is not used elsewhere and for other purposes. Court proceedings relating to divorce, access to children and criminal matters create pressures on clients and therapists to abandon privacy. Confidentiality, a commitment on the part of the therapist for the benefit of the clients, is also seen as the sine qua non of effective casework (Bollas and Sundelson 1995). Confidentiality may be waived by the clients. Disclosure of the content of couple casework requires the informed consent, freely given by both partners. The problematic situations arising out of couples' public domain involvements have led Relate to prepare detailed guidelines about the management of the confidentiality and privacy of couple therapy (Relate 1996).

Confidentiality and privacy also raise taxing issues related to couples' private domains.

> Ayeesha and Robert had been married for 18 months. It was a love match although Ayeesha's family had spoken about making an arranged marriage some years earlier. Robert had become upset and angry at the way Ayeesha's mother, grandmother and aunts attempted to influence every decision the couple needed to take. Discussion about the basis on which therapy might be offered had highlighted the couple's problem. Robert was eager to establish the confidentiality and privacy of the work they were to do but Ayeesha understood 'private' to mean that nothing should be communicated to anyone outside her family. She assured Robert and the therapist that family members would never divulge the couple's affairs to anyone else.

It will be apparent that this situation is very different from those that arise in the public domain, where the nature and implications of privacy and confidentiality are spelled out in statutes, by precedent, or by the explicit terms of a contract. In their private domain, Ayeesha and Robert have different understandings of the idea of privacy deriving from the cultures and value systems of their upbringings. Indeed, they are likely to describe the scope of that domain differently as well. The therapist is faced with a situation in which 'ground rules' for therapy that are usually quite easily negotiated impinge directly on issues that are disrupting the couple relationship. The therapist's duty of care for the relationship, and for the partners as individuals, led to negotiation about an initial phase of therapy based on the partners' agreement that Ayeesha would limit what was communicated to her kinfolk to that which Robert and she agreed was essential in order for her to sustain a good relationship with her family. It was anticipated that the partners' undertaking would raise a range of issues related to expectations about the nature of a couple relationship, about the implications of intimacy, and to do with the scope of the partners' trust in one another. Core beliefs and values were likely to be challenged and the therapist's ethical responsibility would be to monitor differences in the power of the partners and to focus attention on any coersive influences brought to bear on the work to build a couple relationship capable of bridging cultures creatively. That is, the therapist's task was to sustain an ethically appropriate process through which the couple might work out the ethos of their own relationship.

Responsibilities to society

There are a few situations in which a partner or couple may fail to fulfil public domain responsibilities, or may engage in criminal activity, where the therapist has an obligation to ensure that information is passed to the authorities. Child abuse and terrorist activity are examples. However, it is important to differentiate between statutory obligations such as those mentioned, ethical requirements, and therapists' obligations arising out of their work setting and their contracts of employment. For example, a therapist may be obliged to report cases of substance abuse to the client's employer. However, a much wider range of acts of commission or omission which are unlawful, break regulations or conflict with established social norms may come to the attention of therapists and are associated with no such obligations. Those situations may nonetheless evoke powerful responses in the therapist which it might be argued are legitimized by the weight of public opinion and, possibly, the existence of public bodies with responsibilities to bring those involved to book.

> Trevor was divorced after having two children, had relocated and had subsequently set up home with Viv. It was Viv's first long-term relationship. Viv had presented Trevor with an ultimatum: either he contacted the Child Support Agency and began supporting his children or she would end their relationship. She could not be the partner of a man who shirked such an important responsibility. Trevor earned modestly as a 'cash in hand' casual worker on the fringes of the building industry, His ex-wife (had) worked on the checkout of her local supermarket. Trevor believed that the circumstances surrounding his divorce left him with no moral obligation to support the children.

Hearing Trevor and Viv's stories the therapist was immediately in sympathy with Viv's determination to do all she could to get Trevor to act as a responsible parent. It was recognized, nonetheless, that action specifically designed to regularize the situation was the responsibility of the civil authorities and not the therapist. Trevor had 'imported' a significant public domain irregularity into his relationship with Viv. For reasons that were not fully explored, Viv was experiencing that irregularity as disruptive of her private domain relationship with Trevor. It was the nature and consequences of that disruption that needed to be attended to by the couple. A focus on those issues would almost certainly involve the partners in an exploration of their values and priorities, and shed light on the influences that had motivated Trevor to set aside responsibilities and Viv to adopt an 'all or nothing' position regarding her relationship with him.

Thought about in terms of duties of care, Viv and Trevor's situation might appear more complex than those discussed earlier in the chapter. The needs of the relationship, the partners as individuals, the unsupported minors, and society at large, each called for attention. Strictly, the clients are the only persons to whom a duty of care is owed. The third parties are probably best considered to be a cause of concern because of the responsibilities that we all share as members of society – civic responsibilities. It is also important to note that duties of care are not without limitation. It is the therapist's responsibility to recognize those limits and, having done that, to determine what objectives might be negotiated with the couple so as to maximize benefit and minimize harm overall. These are judgements that are made simply and quickly in casework where harm to third parties is not a real concern. It might almost be said that they are made automatically in some cases, but the reality is that, whether or not the interests of third parties (of several different kinds) preoccupy the therapist, all couples bring with them into the consultation room networks of dependent/interdependent relationships to which the couples, and thus the therapist, may need to give consideration at some stage in the therapy.

The work to be done with Viv and Trevor is unlikely to be unusual in nature but their situation does provide a useful illustration of the therapist's need to be clear about the scope and limitations of therapeutic work, and to guard against the inappropriate influence of personal and passionately held views. Ethical judgements are unlikely to be sound when there is a lack of clarity about the nature and range of the therapist's responsibilities.

Emergent issues

It was observed earlier that where a couple relationship can accommodate the partners' differences and celebrate them as a source of strength, the relationship is likely to adapt and adjust to change in circumstance. Much the same can be said of couple therapy itself, and there is no shortage of change in the world of couple relationships. However, a closer analysis of that change indicates that there are a very few absolutely new situations arising in those relationships. It would be more accurate to state that numbers of situations which were formerly rarely met are now more prevalent. To illustrate the ways in which the couple therapist's ethical thinking is required to evolve in response to 'new' critical situations, the impact of three social trends is examined here: growth in diversity within cultural and ethnic groups; the impact of advances in medicine and in the treatment of infertility; and pressures to provide short-term evidence-based therapies.

Diversity and experiment

There is a generally continuing growth in the diversity of attitudes, values and lifestyles found within the cultural and ethnic groups that make up British society. A full analysis of the causes of that growth is subject matter for a sociological study. What is evident is that the socio-economic forces that once disposed individuals and families to conform to the norms of their community are less influential today. There is also a diminution in the valuing of traditional life-choices and lifestyles. Many of yesterday's solutions are demonstrably inappropriate today.

The consequence of these changes is that experiment with life-choices and lifestyles, previously the preserve of adolescence and radical-thinking adults, is now a widespread phenomenon among couples and families of all age groups. This finds expression for the couple therapist in growing numbers of client couples in which partners with different cultural heritages have come together after brief acquaintance. They relate on the basis of shared affiliations to social mores and values which subsequently prove to be superficial and conceal differences of a more profound kind. The partners in such relationships may disown or be only partially aware of the influences that shape their responses to one another. Those whose life-choices are expressions of efforts to find personal adaptations to modern (British) urban society may find efforts to identify and address their heritage attitudes and values threatening and difficult. Couple therapists' awarenesses of the significance to a relationship of those less apparent influences risk undermining their capacity to 'not know' and, in particular, to make false assumptions about the meanings and implications for the partners of key ideas about relationships such as love, intimacy, trust, commitment, family and parenthood. For some such couples there is an engagement in a kind of experimentation with mores and values (sometimes perceived as ill-informed) that is beyond the experience of the therapist.

The ethical challenge for the therapist lies in enabling the couple's exploration and experiment. Much couple casework seeks to assist partners to deal with disruptive issues that are embedded in the framework provided by the couple's relatively stable cultural affiliations. That framework, once understood, gives both partners and therapist reference points against which to test options and evaluate consequences. Where experiment relates to cultural affiliations themselves, reference points need to be validated *by the couple* before being used to test choices about the relationship. The therapeutic process will be interactive and must be freed from the subtle convergent influences that may be exerted by the use of language and ethical thinking grounded in the therapist's culture. The containment offered to the partners will also enable the necessary exploration and experimentation if the assumptions upon which it is based are themselves open to scrutiny and modification.

Medical advances

Growing numbers of couples seeking therapy are dealing with the consequences of the application of medical/surgical techniques that preserve life yet leave the surviving individual a changed person. Though less obvious, involvement in treatments for infertility can precipitate profound change in the partners, especially when that treatment is unsuccessful. Either kind of intervention may be seen as the cause of identity crises for the individuals and for their relationships.

While couple therapists have been making use of medical and psychiatric consultants since the earliest days of the modality's delivery, the medical/surgical interventions that individuals undergo today are of such technical complexity and have such wide-ranging after-effects that the therapist can seldom claim to be aware of all the influences contributing to the crisis being experienced. The issue of competence takes on a new importance. The feasibility and nature of working as part of an interdisciplinary team needs constant re-examination. Significantly, gaining a realistic appreciation about what things can be changed, those things that *might* be changed, and the things that must be accepted as unchangeable becomes a pressing matter, yet one on which neither partners nor therapist may be able to obtain reliable advice. The extent of the partners' trauma may thus be beyond estimation and the eventual outcomes quite uncertain.

From an ethical standpoint, the fact that the couple may *not* be the experts on their own relationship, and that circumstances, the partners, and their relationship may change in dramatic and unforeseen ways, present new challenges. Dealing with not knowing, and perhaps a reliance on others outside the consulting room, becomes the task of both the therapist and the partners. This places a great emphasis on the present and the processing of the partners' thoughts, feelings and any new information available to them. Containment must have a priority, and that will almost inevitably oblige the therapist to make full use of reflexivity and supervision since the duty of care will call on a full measure of the therapist's *personal moral qualities* (BACP 2002). The ethical preoccupation of the therapist is thus on ensuring that they are fully available to the partners as a professional worker.

Short-term evidence-based therapy

Client expectations, the commercial pressures of the delivery of managed care, and more general pressures to *demonstrate* the (cost)-effectiveness of a form of therapy, all impinge on the therapist when negotiating the form, content and duration of the therapy to be provided for a couple. Those influences have grown in recent years, and continue to grow. One of the claims that has been made for couple therapy for many years is that, as well as assisting couples to resolve immediate problems, it also offers the couple the opportunity to gain the awarenesses and learn the skills needed to serve as one another's partners in a continuing therapeutic relationship through which both the relationship and the individuals thrive. Couple therapists will be aware of the anecdotal evidence they have accumulated that this secondary benefit is achievable, though no substantial research study is known that confirms the fact. While not discounting the power of brief therapeutic interventions, it is arguable that therapy limited to a very few sessions offers limited opportunities to couples to acquire those capacities.

The evidence base assembled for 'effective' therapies is typically derived from short-term studies of the benefits gained by clients (Tolley and Rowland 1995). The secondary benefits of couple therapy, believed to be significant, demand longitudinal studies spanning the duration of the focal relationships. None is known. The couple therapist is thus badly placed to argue for extended forms of therapy though possibly personally persuaded that numbers of their clients' relationships would benefit significantly from that kind of intervention.

There is thus an ethical dilemma to be faced by the couple therapist. While waiting lists have fluctuated, no evidence is known which suggests that the availability of couple therapy exceeds overall demand. (It must be acknowledged that since much of couple therapy has shifted from availability at nominal charge to supply at cost, demand has reduced, but that may be a matter of inadequate education and marketing rather than a lessening of need.) Potentially, couple therapists have the option to negotiate forms and durations of therapy that address less tractable relationship problems and result in the secondary benefits described. Couple therapists are thus challenged ethically when determining the setting (private, voluntary, commercial) in which they provide their service, and by the constraints which each of those settings impose on their freedom to negotiate with partners therapeutic interventions which it is judged best match their needs.

Couple therapy has a long and honourable history. Today's client relationships are undeniably more demanding than those met a quarter of a century ago. In part that has to do with shifts in what is viewed to be the public and private domain of couples' relationships. It is also to do with the new opportunities and challenges that couples face. Fundamentally, the task of the couple therapist remains the same: providing a trusted environment in which partners can risk a full involvement in efforts to find ways to engage in creative and enriching, committed intimate relationships – a primary human need – and thereby realize their personal potential. The primary ethical obligation of the couple therapist is to enable unique individuals living in similarly unique social contexts to strive towards those ends.

Notes

1. Here 'couple therapy' is used to refer to a wide variety of kinds of couple counselling and couple psychotherapy. Psychoanalytic marital psychotherapy together with services offered by analysts and analytical psychologists will not be addressed specifically though having some characteristics in common with other more generally available services.
2. The individuals described in this chapter's vignettes are fictional. The situations illustrated are drawn directly from the author's casework experience.

References

BACP (2002) *Ethical Framework for Good Practice in Counselling and Psychotherapy*. Rugby: British Association for Counselling and Psychotherapy.

Bannister, K. and Pincus, L. (1965) *Shared Phantasy in Marital Problems: Therapy in a Four-Person Relationship*. London: Institute of Marital Studies, The Tavistock Institute of Human Relations.

Bennun, I. (1984) Evaluating marital therapy: a hospital and community study, *British Journal of Guidance and Counselling*, 12: 84–91.

Bockus, F. (1993) *Couple Therapy*. North Vale: Aronson.

Bollas, C. and Sundelson, D. (1995) *The New Informants*. London: Karnac.

Bornstein, P. and Bornstein, M. (1986) *Marital Therapy: A Behavioural-Communications Approach*. New York: Pergamon.

Brown, R. (1999) *Imago Relationship Therapy: An Introduction to Theory and Practice*. New York: Wiley.

Bubenzer, D. and West, J. (1993) *Counselling Couples*. London: Sage.

Burnham, J. (1986) *Family Therapy*. London: Tavistock.

Butler, C. and Joyce, V. (1998) *Counselling Couples in Relationships: An Introduction to the Relate Approach*. Chichester: Wiley.

Carter, B. and McGoldrick, M. (eds) (1989) *The Changing Family Life Cycle: A Framework for Family Therapy*, 2nd edn. Boston: Allyn & Bacon.

Casement, P. (1985) *On Learning from the Patient*. London: Tavistock.

Chasin, R., Grunebaum, H. and Herzig, M. (eds) (1990) *One Couple: Four Realities*. New York: Guilford Press.

Clark, D. and Haldane, D. (1990) *Wedlocked*. Cambridge: Polity Press.

Clarkson, P. (1995) *The Therapeutic Relationship*. London: Whurr.

Clulow, C. (1985) *Marital Therapy: An Inside View*. Aberdeen: Aberdeen University Press.

Clulow, C. (ed.) (2001) *Adult Attachment and Couple Psychotherapy*. London: Brunner–Routledge.

Crane, D. (1996) *Fundamentals of Marital Therapy*. New York: Brunner/Mazel.

Crowe, M. (1978) Conjoint marital therapy: a controlled outcome study, *Psychological Medicine*, 8: 623–36.

Dicks, H. (1967) *Marital Tensions*. London: Routledge & Kegan Paul.

Egan, G. (1975) *The Skilled Helper: Model, Skills, and Methods for Effective Helping*, 2nd edn. Monterey, CA: Brooks/Cole.

Fisher, J. (1999) *The Uninvited Guest: Emerging from Narcissism towards Marriage*. London: Karnac.

Flaskas, C. (2002) *Family Therapy beyond Postmodernism: Practice Challenges Theory*. Hove: Brunner–Routledge.

Flaskas, C. and Perlesz, A. (eds) (1996) *The Therapeutic Relationship in Systemic Therapy*. London: Karnac.

Fonagy, P. (2001) *Attachment Theory and Psychoanalysis*. New York: Other Press.

Freeman, D. (1982) *Marital Crisis and Short-term Counselling: A Casebook*. London: Free Press.

Gilbert, M. and Shmukler, D. (1996) *Brief Therapy with Couples: An Integrative Approach*. Chichester: Wiley.

Guiver, P. (1973) *The Trouble Sharers: Counselling in Personal Relationships*. Rugby: National Marriage Guidance Council.

Gurman, A. (ed.) (1985) *Casebook of Marital Therapy*. New York: Guilford Press.

Guthrie, L. and Mattinson, J. (1971) *Brief Casework with a Marital Problem*. London: Institute of Marital Studies, The Tavistock Institute of Human Relations.

Hooper, D. (1985) Marital therapy: an overview of research, in W. Dryden (ed.) *Marital Therapy in Britain. Vol. 2: Special Areas*. London: Harper & Row.

Hooper, D. and Roberts, J. (1967) *Disordered Lives: An Interpersonal Account*. Rugby: National Marriage Guidance Council.

Jacobson, N. and Christensen, A. (1996) *Acceptance and Change in Couple*

Therapy: A Therapist's Guide to Transforming Relationships. New York: Norton.

Jacobson, N. and Margolin, G. (1979) *Marital Therapy: Strategies based on Social Learning and Behaviour Exchange Principles*. New York: Brunner/ Mazel.

James, A. and Wilson, K. (1986) *Couples, Conflict and Change*. London: Tavistock.

Johnson, S. and Greenberg, L. (eds) (1994) *The Heart of the Matter: Perspectives on Emotion in Marital Therapy*. New York: Brunner/Mazel.

Lewis, J., Clark, D. and Morgan, D. (1992) *Whom God hath Joined Together: The Work of Marriage Guidance*. London: Routledge.

Mace, D. (1972) *Sexual Difficulties in Marriage*. Rugby: National Marriage Guidance Council.

Mattinson, J. (1975) *The Reflection Process in Casework Supervision*. London: Institute of Marital Studies, The Tavistock Institute of Human Relations.

McCarthy, P., Walker, J. and Kain, J. (1998) *Telling It As It Is: The Client Experience of Relate Counselling*. Report by the Newcastle Centre for Family Studies, University of Newcastle upon Tyne.

McNamee, S. and Gergen, K. (eds) (1992) *Therapy as Social Construction*. London: Sage.

Mearns, D. and Thorne, B. (1988) *Person-centred Counselling in Action*. London: Sage.

Pincus, L. (ed.) (1960) *Marriage: Studies in Emotional Conflict and Growth*. London: Institute of Marital Studies, The Tavistock Institute of Medical Psychology.

Pincus, L. and Dare, C. (1978) *Secrets in the Family*. London: Faber & Faber.

Rabin, C. (1996) *Equal Partners: Good Friends*. London: Routledge.

Relate (1996) *Confidentiality: Principles and Practice in Marital and Couple Counselling and in Psychosexual Therapy*, 2nd edn. Rugby: Relate.

Rogers, C. (1942) *Counselling and Psychotherapy: Newer Concepts in Practice*. New York: Houghton-Mifflin.

Rogers, C. (1957) The necessary and sufficient conditions of therapeutic personality change, *Journal of Consulting Psychology*, 21(2): 99.

Rogers, C. (1973) *Becoming Partners: Marriage and its Alternatives*. London: Constable.

Ruszczynski, S. (ed.) (1993) *Psychotherapy with Couples*. London: Karnac.

Scharff, D. and Scharff, J. (1991) *Object Relations Couple Therapy*. Northvale, NJ: Aronson.

Tolley, K. and Rowland, N. (1995) *Evaluating the Cost-effectiveness of Counselling in Health Care*. London: Routledge.

Truax, C. and Carkhuff, R. (1967) *Towards Effective Counselling and Psychotherapy: Training and Practice*. Chicago: Aldine.

Venables, E. (1971) *Counselling*. Rugby: National Marriage Guidance Council.

Weeks, G. and Hof, L. (eds) (1994) *The Marital-relationship Therapy Casebook: Theory and Application of the Intersystem Model*. New York: Brunner/Mazel.

Willi, J. (1982) *Couples in Collusion: The Unconscious Dimension in Partner Relationships*. Claremont: Hunter House.

Willi, J. (1984) *Dynamics of Couples Therapy: The Uses of the Concept of Collusion and its Application to the Therapeutic Triangle*. Northvale, NJ: Aronson.

6 Ethical issues in marital and family counselling in India

Lina Kashyap

In any society, family counselling services can be examined only with reference to the context within which they are being offered. Therefore this chapter first highlights Indian social realities with reference to couple and family relations. It then discusses the characteristics of marital and family counselling services in the country and describes some critical situations in which ethical issues and dilemmas are faced by contemporary Indian counsellors. Lastly, emergent issues in this field are presented.

Couple and family relations in India

India is a vast country which is multicultural, multilingual and multireligious. Hence families in India reflect the diversity, complexity, cultural and religious traditions based on caste and class that are part of the Indian ethos. They also reflect the changes brought about in their structure by the impact of globalization and modernization on Indian society which has further marginalized some sectors of society and pushed more families below the poverty line. At present, Indian families are in a state of transition as they grapple with issues related to continuity and change.

Indian families have some distinctive characteristics when compared with western families. In most parts of India, families are patriarchal in structure and ideology; roles and responsibilities, and control and distribution of resources are strictly determined by age, sex and generation. Interpersonal communication between members of the family is also highly influenced by hierarchy based on sex, age and kin. Such a system places a high premium on upholding family dignity and status in society and family unity and cohesiveness. Elaborate rituals convey the message that family bonds are immutable, dependable and lifelong (Mullatti 1995; Bharat 1997). Today, this hierarchy is being questioned by the educated, earning young members of the family who are demanding democratization of family roles and distribution of family resources.

In the past, the 'ideal' family pattern was three-generational, with the eldest male member heading his family. There has been a gradual change in the family structure of both urban and rural India towards a more nuclear pattern resulting in a trend towards democratization of family norms. However, even in nuclear families, the perception and practice of marital roles by both husband and wife are still sex-based (Desai 1991).

Even today, in the name of familism, children are socialized quite early into concepts of inequality by sex and age. Boys are considered as economic assets, and many parental aspirations rest in them. They are indulged from an early age and grow up carefree and psychologically secure. The young daughter's socialization, on the other hand, is designed to equip her for the demands of her adult roles as wife and daughter-in-law. On attaining puberty, she is faced with her parents' anxiety about finding a marriage partner and her own uncertainty about the type of marital home she will enter. In a family system that remains patriarchal, partrilineal and patrilocal, young women have a subordinate status first in their parental and later in their marital families. Heavy demands are made in both homes in terms of housework and socially appropriate behaviour. Norms of segregation of women are still rigid (Kashyap 2000a).

Nevertheless, social and legislative reforms have opened up greater opportunities for women that have enabled them to seek higher education and gainful employment outside the home. Educated working women, especially those from the higher castes and classes, are beginning to acquire higher status in the family. This in turn has influenced their perception of themselves and their different roles. It has changed their aspirations and expectations of marriage and their marital partner. At the same time, their changing status and new assertiveness has created ripples in their family life because, while women have attempted to change their roles to a great extent, men have changed their roles only a little, and the broader workplace and cultural norms have not changed much at all.

Marriage in India is perceived as a socio-religious institution rather than a personal relationship because it takes place between two families rather than two individuals. Indian marriages are still generally arranged by parents and members of the kinship group with class and caste positions and religion being important considerations. Traditionally, individuals were expected to marry within their own caste and religious group, and even today this norm is widely practised. Although patterns of partner selection vary in terms of extent of choice given to the young man or woman, family approval is essential for the marriage to take place.

Hindu marriages are considered a sacrament, not just a contract, and therefore the fulfilment of a family's needs. Ensuring family cohesion at all costs takes precedence over individual compatibility and individual fulfilment. This perspective has affected the development of marriage as a personal relationship.

While young couples still perceive the family as the foundation of Indian society and marriage as the centrepoint of family life, the traditional perception of marriage as a social obligation for the perpetuation of lineage is gradually being replaced by the concept of marriage for love, companionship and individual happiness. In fact, young couples are at the crossroads as they try to balance traditional beliefs and practices with modern concepts and values.

Most couples in India start their marital life in the house of the husband's parents. As most marriages are arranged, the couple has to move from commitment to the marriage to commitment to the marital relationship. In the process, the couple has to negotiate expectations, roles and patterns of behaviour not only between themselves, but also individually and together with both the family units. In the patrilocal family system it is the new bride who enters her husband's family as a new member. She therefore has to make adjustments to meet the needs and expectations of not only her spouse but also those of his relatives. Adjustment by the wife to her in-laws is very important in the Indian context as lack of support and acceptance by these new relatives on the one hand, and active interference by them in the marital relationship on the other, are major factors leading to marital conflict.

Some of the problems in marriage faced by Indian couples are similar to those faced by couples anywhere in the world, such as: alcoholism or drug addiction of spouse; infidelity; desertion; verbal, physical or sexual abuse of spouse; and sexual incompatibility.

However, some of the distinctive factors that impinge on Indian marriages are socio-culturally based, such as childlessness or no sons (Kawale 1985; Pothen 1986; Chaudhary 1988), dowry demands (cash, jewellery and luxury articles) by in-laws (Ghadially and Kumar 1988; Bhatti 1990; Parihar 1990), breaking down or weakening of kinship networks, and interference by immediate and/or extended family members who exert power and control over the couple as a unit or individually on the husband or wife in a manner which is destructive to the marital relationship (Bhatt and Surti 1979; Ghadially and Kumar 1988; Kashyap 2000b). Macro realities such as globalization and economic liberalization have increased aspiration for material goods but reduced the family's buying power.

Characteristics of marital and family counselling services

One can say that advice related to marriage and family matters in India has been an age-old practice as it finds reference in many Indian folklore, epic poems and religious scriptures. However, such advice on family matters used traditionally to be offered by elder family members and kin as these matters have always been treated as a private domain. The emphasis in such advice was usually on maintaining the family bond at all costs.

The notion of seeking help from somebody outside the family for family matters was alien to Indian society for a long time. Marriage and family counselling as a professional intervention in India is a recent phenomenon. Although there is now less stigma attached to seeking professional counselling, it is still almost the last resort after the family's own efforts at reconciliation have failed and when family equilibrium is threatened.

Marriage and family counselling is offered in a variety of settings. Many voluntary organizations (VOs) for women and children offer a range of services including marital counselling. Counsellors in secondary settings such as schools, colleges, hospitals, private medical and health settings, and social service departments of industries have also been offering marital and family counselling whenever required. However, there are very few VOs that focus exclusively on marital and family counselling.

Often the persons offering counselling services in all these settings are medical practitioners, psychiatrists, psychologists and social workers, most of whom have had some basic training in counselling. Besides these professionals, voluntary workers with an 'interest' in this area but no training also offer counselling in some of these settings based on their own life experiences.

The 1980s saw two developments that gave some impetus to the development of marriage and family counselling services in India. One of the innovations in state interventions was the enactment of the Family Court Act in 1984. One of the court's distinctive features is the absence of legal practitioners and the appointment of counsellors holding a master's degree in social sciences or social work and having a minimum of two years' experience in family counselling. While the family courts have had a better rate of recovery of maintenance than the regular courts, they have had a limited impact on the whole as they are too few in number and they are located in only a few urban areas. It must be added here that while the establishment of family courts has speeded up the legal proceedings, the route to filing a case in the court is still a very turbulent process for many women.

The second development in the 1980s was the initiation by the government of a grant-in-aid scheme to voluntary organizations for running family counselling centres (FCCs). These centres were expected to provide a range of preventive, curative and rehabilitative services such as counselling in family maladjustment, reconciliation in cases of marital disputes, out-of-court settlements in family disputes, investigation in dowry death cases and domestic violence. These centres were also expected to provide appropriate referral services.

The VOs which have undertaken to run the FCCs under the grant-in-aid scheme are diverse: from grass-root organizations involved with urban and rural development, those offering specific social services, to those working exclusively on issues related to women's development and those offering specialized counselling services. Thus the FCC is often not the only service offered by these VOs. In addition, because of the very low remuneration offered to the counsellors working in these FCCs, one finds in many cases that the personnel working as counsellors in these FCCs are really laypeople who have no systematic training in marriage and family counselling.

There is no statutory body regulating marital and family counselling services in the country. In recent years, counsellors in family courts and practising family therapists have formed their own associations. A code of ethics for professional social workers was drawn up and widely circulated by the Tata Institute of Social Sciences. Subsequently, in 2002, the Bombay Association of Trained Social Workers revised it to its present form as the Declaration of Ethics for Professional Social Workers (see Appendix 3 to this book). This declaration contains a value framework regarding ethical responsibility to self and profession, to the marginalized and other people in need, to society and state, to co-workers and employing organizations, and to social work research. In the writer's understanding, medical practitioners, including psychiatrists, follow the ethical standards laid down by the Indian Medical Council.

There are very few professional counsellors in private practice in India, and most counsellors are salaried employees in voluntary welfare organizations. Their clientele, whether individuals or families, are generally from the lower socio-economic classes and are frequently struggling with financial, physical and psychological problems which compound the counsellor's task of their rehabilitation. However, in recent years, there is a growing acceptance of the need to seek professional counselling in family matters among the educated population of Indian society.

One of the major problems faced by VOs in this field is lack of trained counsellors. At present, although there are a few diploma and degree courses in the general area of counselling, there are no educational institutions in India offering a comprehensive specialized training programme in marriage and family counselling. A few of the current practitioners have trained abroad, generally in the USA and UK, and a few others have undergone short-term training programmes of up to a fortnight in this field. The writer has herself conducted such programmes in different parts of the country for laypersons appointed as counsellors in FCCs in order to expose them to basic counselling skills. Most practitioners in this field have received no specialized training for their work and have had to learn and improvise as they worked.

An overview of Indian research on marital counselling by Mane (1991) has revealed that there were very few research-based articles on the subject and that what was available had a psychiatric orientation, i.e. when one of the partners, usually the wife, has developed somatic, psychosomatic or psychiatric symptoms, and when marital conflict is identified as the predisposing factor. The lack of research interest in marital interaction, roles and power in the Indian context is in itself not surprising as problems related to family dynamics and marital disharmony are still treated as private matters to be kept within the family, and there continues to be a conspiracy of silence about the nature of unequal power relations within the family and within the marital relationship (Ramu 1988).

In terms of approaches used by practitioners, few practitioners have been reported to be using psychotherapy with individual clients when working with and attempting to alter the interpersonal variables as they present themselves in the counselling situation (Davar 2001).

Mohan's (1972) analysis based on researches conducted at the All India Institute of Medical Sciences, New Delhi, points out that didactic/directive therapy was used most often, in which the techniques utilized were use of authority, suggestions and advice and where the goal of therapy was to foster adjustment and encourage interdependence. Conjoint rather than concurrent therapy was used more often with couples, as the former was viewed with more acceptance by the *husband* (Mohan 1972; Channabasavanna and Bhatti 1985). To handle the impact of family dynamics on the marital relationship, key family members from both sides of the family have been involved in the counselling sessions to exploit the strength of the family as a unit for ending marital disharmony (Mohan 1972). This analysis, however, does not acknowledge the role of the family unit in creating marital problems.

Channabasavanna and Bhatti's (1985) study of 30 women who had neurotic symptoms examines the process of therapy in the context of the western-based role expectation model which views the role played by the spouses in marriage as being based on socially shared expectations about it. The focus of the therapy was seen to be understanding the quality of the marital relationship and the relationship between the family of orientation and the couple. The major intervention strategies seemed to be geared towards orienting the couple to understand how their conflict is linked to their family of orientation and that it is not a manifestation of individual problems alone.

Critical situations and their ethical resolution

Generally speaking, the counsellors are from the middle class/upper castes. In this situation, the values and belief systems of the clients and counsellors may differ. Hence an ethical concern for Indian counsellors is to be conscious and cautious that caste and class issues do not interfere with their ability to work with their clients but actually contribute to their understanding of issues, and to guard against paternalistic attitudes towards them.

The ideological base and perspective of the organization often dictates the kinds of interventions that counsellors are able to make, which is another area of concern. For example, when an agency's goals in dealing with couples in marital conflict is reconciliation and when the agency measures the counsellor's success or ability by the number of reconciliation's they have achieved, counsellors may become pressured to place the agency's goals above their clients' interests and right to self-determination. A similar situation also arises in specialized agencies such as family courts, where the emphasis is on conciliation between the concerned parties as far as possible, aimed at preserving the institution of marriage.

Heavy caseloads do not provide counsellors in India with the luxury of having more than a few sessions with each client or being more than a co-therapist with a colleague. Also, counsellors are often so overwhelmed by the caseload and the variety of tasks they have to carry out in primary and secondary settings that the quantity of their work sometimes outweighs the quality of their output. This has also led to burnout symptoms, reducing the level of efficiency of the counsellor or causing a high turnover of counselling staff. All these situations have affected the development of sound ethical counselling practice.

In specialized agencies such as family courts, counsellors have been provided with a lot of power, their report is confidential and cannot be cross-examined. However, the report is also not binding on the judges. This situation, as Mitra (2000) has rightly pointed out, trivializes even the serious job of counsellor intervention. In the writer's experience, this situation has adversely affected the motivation and commitment of the family court counsellors to the counselling process, which in turn has affected their effectiveness and credibility in the eyes of the client system and the judiciary, as well as in their own view.

The FCC scheme has mandated the appointment of two counsellors and provides for their salaries. However, as the salary scales are very low, financially dependent organizations have been compromising in terms of recruitment of counsellors, by appointing young, inexperienced, untrained counsellors, who have had no exposure to family and marital problems. Moreover, in the name of counselling, what is actually offered is simply advice with hardly any therapeutic element. In cases of marital conflict, most FCCs have taken a conservative approach of maintaining the status quo about the inviolability of the family unit at the cost of the well-being of individual family members. This raises serious questions about what is achieved in these centres, apart from referral to available support services. The author recalls one of the counsellors telling her how she had 'successfully' handled a case of sexual assault of a 16-year-old girl. When the mother and daughter had come to see her she had advised them to immediately get an abortion and urged the mother to get her daughter married as soon as possible. She then gave them the address of an abortion clinic and a marriage bureau.

There is an urgent need for the in-service training and ongoing professional supervision of these counsellors that calls for active campaigning by the professional community for this change in policy. Although both the Family Court Act and the FCC scheme have clauses about providing ongoing training and supervision, only token attention has been paid to this critical issue.

The brief review of available research studies mentioned in the earlier section has pointed to the use of largely western intervention models without much indigenization for addressing Indian realities. The western orientation of focusing only on the couple and their status roles and emotional interaction without reference to the structural power imbalance in couples and families that actually determines the nature of emotional relationships between the partners, is ineffective in the Indian context. However, this is not to discount the value of couple counselling per se.

Based on this review and the writer's own observations in the field, it seems that much of professional intervention involving couples and families continues to accommodate the implacable, entrenched position men often take in therapy by forcing the socially powerless, resourceless woman to change and adjust to prescribed roles. This is disheartening as it merely serves to maintain the status quo and does not resolve the conflict in the long run.

Emergent issues

There is no doubt that today's Indian family is indeed ready and in great need of marital and family counselling therapy (Oommen

2000). However, in the writer's view, shared by a few contemporary counsellors in India, the development of this field in India has to follow a radically different course from that taken by western countries.

First of all, it is necessary to make a major shift in conceptualizing the nature of counselling intervention and social problems by acknowledging that unequal power relations (taking material, emotional or ideological forms) are the basis of social injustice (McNay 1992). To elaborate, the nature and role of patriarchal power relations in all spheres of Indian family life, including couple relationships, and the power some women in the family have over other women, needs to be recognized and understood. The problems of most couples cannot be rationally addressed or resolved until the core inequalities of their relationship are acknowledged and addressed (Carter 1992; Vindhya 2001).

It is also necessary to reconsider a more integrated understanding of the nature of problems faced by couples and families and develop a form of counselling practice based on a synthesis of structural and individual (personal) perspectives. The most significant work in integrating the structural and individual levels of analysis, the personal and the political, has been carried out by feminists (McNay 1992; Hill and Ballon 1998; Shah 2001).

The feminist perspective recognizes that much of the distress that people face is socio-culturally based. It provides an understanding of the patriarchal social context, of the unequal distribution of power, of the socially structured and culturally maintained patterns of man/woman relations, and the manner in which they affect interpersonal relationships within the family, especially spousal relationships (Hill and Ballon 1998; Vindhya 2001).

The systemic nature of couple and family difficulties in India is more pronounced than in many other societies. Systems theory describes how values in the wider society interact with social institutions like the family and the ways in which the distribution of power in macro structures is reflected and reinforced in microstructures like the family. Hence, given the power and significance of the family system in India, integration of the feminist perspective and some aspects of the systems theory can help in the development of a broader theoretical framework for understanding inequality and the use of power relations as a basis for intervention. Only within such a framework can marriage and family counselling incorporate a sex-sensitive, systemic view of families. Moreover, as Oommen (2000) suggests, in order for Indians to overcome both the alienation of individualism and the tyranny of collectivism, a balance must be struck.

During the 1980s and 1990s, feminist activism in India attempted to raise awareness about the role of patriarchal power relations in all spheres of life and to challenge social institutions and other cultural and political structures that have a direct bearing on women's lives and well-being. At about the same time, a few other professionals from different disciplines working with women's organizations began to give a similar conceptual and intervention basis to increasing women's awareness of socio-political pressures, encouraging their respect for themselves and other women, and helping them to recognize their choices and their right to change the context of their lives.

One such effort was made by the writer's colleagues from the Department of Social Work at the Tata Institute of Social Sciences, in the form of an experimental field action project for demonstrating a sex-sensitive approach to deal with violence against women, including domestic violence.

The Special Cell for Women and Children, a joint venture of a university department and the Mumbai Police, which began in one police station in Mumbai, has successfully demonstrated a strategy of working with the state system on the issue of violence against women and has now established several cells across the state of Maharashtra. It has developed an effective model of practice for working with women who have encountered physical, emotional or sexual violence within the family and community. Its documentation has become a rich resource material for sex-sensitive social work teaching and training in India.

In the two decades of the work of the special cells, the social workers who provide the counselling services have struggled to deal with several emergent issues, a few of which are highlighted here.

The social workers at the special cells have mostly been young women with a master's degree in social work. They have been subject to the same patriarchal ethos as their women clients and they too have been socialized to preserve the sanctity of the family at all costs. However, their professional training has told them to challenge the structural power imbalance within families and within the marital relationship. This raises a dilemma for some of them, as addressing the issue of sex inequality publicly may also mean threatening the status quo in their personal lives.

The sex of the social worker certainly makes a difference, according to some social workers, who feel that no matter how balanced a woman social worker is, the male client tends to perceive that her effort has been solely for the woman's benefit. Male social workers have found it easier to build rapport with the police and with male clients. However, probably what matters most is the maturity of the counsellor and their ability to communicate effectively with clients, which also means speaking in the clients' language, being sensitive to their religious and cultural background, and being able to imbibe and then to transfer to the clients the newer values of equity and human dignity.

As a counselling strategy, taking up a position of clinical value neutrality in situations such as violence against women may in fact re-victimize the victim and re-establish the status quo of the sexes, vindicating male aggression and chauvinism in relationships. Therefore, social workers at the special cell have taken a pro-women stand in their work, while taking care not to lose sight of the principle of having a non-judgemental attitude in terms of accepting and managing ethnic and religious differences in their clients.

On the issue of confidentiality, their concern on the one hand has been to take care of the individual's basic right to privacy. At the same time, because domestic violence is not merely an individual problem but also a social phenomenon, their concern has also been how to universalize this issue and bring it from the personal to the political arena.

The special cell counsellors are expected to have a firm belief in the principle of client self-determination. However, they have admitted that operationalizing this in their practice has been a hard struggle for themselves and their female clients; extremely difficult because the women who come to them are defenseless, powerless and may have rarely been given an opportunity to take decisions for themselves or express their views on any issue. They have therefore first to help their women clients to feel supported and not alone without any alternatives, and next to encourage them to take decisions that are informed and carefully reasoned and not purely emotional. However, they have not always succeeded in this endeavour and they find themselves in a dilemma when the violated woman decides to go back to a situation that they and the woman know to be life threatening, but they still have to allow the client to make her own decision.

> A joint meeting with family members from the husband's and wife's families and the elders of their religious community (Jammat) was in session in the presence of the counsellor. All were trying to convince Salma to return to her marriage. Within a span of 20 minutes Salma told the counsellor, 'I don't want a divorce. I am going back with my husband.' Yet in a previous individual session Salma had expressed her anger and resentment towards her husband and in-laws who were torturing her. She stated that her marital relationship held no meaning for her any more. Her husband has taken a second wife as well. She had taken a bold decision to separate after considering all her choices and had earlier declined the option of reconciliation. After conversing with the Jammat, she decided to reunite with her husband and informed the counsellor that she would come back to her in future if necessary.

Thus although the counsellor realized that the client's decision was more emotional than a result of rational thinking, she had to accept the client's decision on this issue.

As an educator and practitioner, the writer has been concerned for quite some time about the limitations of purely western-based models and theories for handling newer problems related to contemporary marriage and family counselling in India, and also the paucity of professionally rigorous training programmes in this field. Keeping in mind the immense need and scope for marital and family counselling in India, in 1999 she began to put together a team of experienced faculty members, mostly from schools of social work from different parts of the country. This team has been working on developing an India-specific core curriculum on marriage and family counselling and documenting it in the form of an edited book. The plan is to be able simultaneously to offer this standardized curriculum through the universities to which the team members belong in order to achieve a national coverage of a larger population. Separate training modules would be offered to existing counsellors for upgrading their skills, to new entrants in this field, and to faculty members from the disciplines of social work and psychology as trainers. However, with the development of training programmes, there will have to be a simultaneous development of accreditation and licensing bodies to ensure ethical counselling practice. This is going to be an enormous task. India has a long way to go and many miles to cover, but the important point is that the journey has begun.

References

Bharat, S. (1997) Family socialization of the Indian child, *Trends in Social Science Research* 4(1): 201–16.

Bhatt, K. and Surti, K.N. (1979) A correlational study of marital and family adjustment, *Indian Journal of Clinical Psychology*, 6(1): 33–58.

Bhatti, R.S. (1990) Socio-cultural dynamics of wife battering, in S. Sood (ed.) *Violence Against Women*. Jaipur: Arihant.

Carter, B. (1992) Stonewalling feminism, *The Family Therapy Networker*, 16(1): 64–9.

Channabasavanna, S.M. and Bhatti, R.S. (1985) Utility of 'roles and expectation model' on understanding the 'quality of marital life' and treatment of marital problems, *Indian Journal of Social Psychiatry*, 1(2): 105–20.

Chaudhary, J.N. (1988) *Divorce in Indian Society*. Jaipur: Rupa Books.

Davar, B. (2001) *Mental Health from a Gender Perspective*. New Delhi: Sage.

Desai, M. (1991) Research on families with marital problems: review and implications, *Research on Families with Problems in India*, Vol. II. Mumbai: Unit for Family Studies, TISS.

Ghadially, R. and Kumar, P. (1988) Bride burning: the psycho-social dynamics of dowry deaths, in R. Ghadially (ed.) *Women in Indian Society*. New Delhi: Sage.

Hill, M. and Ballon (1998) Making therapy feminist: a practice survey, in M. Hill (ed.) *Feminist Therapy as a Political Act*. Binghamton: The Harrington Press.

Kashyap, L. (2000a) India: university and technical institute students in Mumbai, in J. Gibson-Cline (ed.) *Youth and Coping in Twelve Nations: Surveys of 18–20 year old people*. London: Routledge.

Kashyap, L. (2000b) Meeting the needs of families with marital problems in the changing Indian society, in M. Koschorke (ed.) *What Produces Change? The Forces Impacting on Relationships*. Berlin-Wannsee: International Commission on Marriage and Interpersonal Relations.

Kawale, K.G. (1985) Divorce problems: a sociological study. Doctoral dissertation, Marathwada University.

Mane, P. (1991) Research on marital counselling and therapy in India: relevance and priorities for Indian practice, *Research on Families with Problems in India: Issues and Implications*. Vol. II. Mumbai: Unit for Family Studies, TISS.

McNay, M. (1992) Social work and power relations: towards a framework for an integrated practice, in M. Langan and L. Day (eds) *Women, Oppression and Social Work: Issues in Anti-discriminatory Practice*. London: Routledge.

Mitra, N. (2000) Domestic violence as a public issue: a review of responses. Mumbai: Unit for Women's Studies, TISS.

Mohan, D. (1972) *Pre-marriage and Marriage Counselling in the Indian Family in the Change and Challenge of the Seventies*. New Delhi: Indian Social Institute.

Mullatti, L. (1995) Families in India: beliefs and realities, *Journal of Comparative Family Studies*, 26(1): 11–25.

Oommen, T.K. (2000) Family therapy: challenging the system. *Hindu*, March 26.

Parihar, L. (1990) Battered wife syndrome: some socio-legal aspects, in S. Sood (ed.) *Violence against Women*, pp. 35–44. Jaipur: Arihant.

Pothen, S. (1986) *Divorce: Its Causes and Consequences in Hindu Society*. Delhi: Shakti Books.

Ramu, G. (1988) Marital roles and power: perceptions and reality in the urban setting, *Journal of Comparative Family Studies*, 19(2): 207–228.

Shah, A. (2001) Gender issues in mental health: a clinical psychology perspective, in B. Davar (ed.) *Mental Health from a Gender Perspective*. New Delhi: Sage.

Vindhya, U. (2001) From the personal to the collective: psychological/feminist issues of women's mental health, in B. Darar (ed.) *Mental Health from a Gender Perspective*. New Delhi: Sage.

7 Ethical thinking in family therapy

John Burnham, Suzanne Cerfontyne and Joan Wynn

Characteristics

We share with other therapeutic approaches common values and goals aimed at facilitating healing and freeing clients to 'move on' with their lives. Working with family groups raises some interesting and important ethical issues, which may not apply when working with individuals. This chapter outlines and explores some of these issues and proposes ways of addressing them in an open and transparent way.

Like other therapeutic modalities, family therapy is required to show its effectiveness. Evidence-based studies indicate that this way of working is effective in a range of problems, across the lifespan and in a variety of contexts: see, for example, Hubble *et al.* (1999) for an overview of what works, and Carr (2000a,b) for an up-to-date review in both child- and adult-focused issues. Research skills are seen as a vital tool in creating and maintaining an ethical practice, and so including research in training is seen as important (see Association for Family Therapy 1999: Learning outcomes 16 'An ability to critically evaluate relevant research findings' and 17 'Sufficient knowledge of research methods to be able to plan and carry out a piece of research relevant to the field'). The case for family therapists as 'scientist-practitioners' is outlined in Crane and Hafen (2002).

Training undertaken by a typical practitioner

Training programmes include theory and clinical practice and are four years in length. Most applicants will have a qualification in one of the helping professions. A distinctive aspect of the training is the team approach and the use of live supervision via a one-way screen or videotape link-up. This creates opportunities to utilize systemic concepts such as collaboration, multiple perspectives and transparency, which can enrich the service offered to clients (see Hoffman 1981). Another strength is that the resources of a team can generate multiple perspectives upon any situation that may pose an ethical dilemma.

> A therapist in training has developed a prejudice, arising from life experiences, family stories, personal and professional scripts, which could potentially lead to ethical dilemmas in clinical practice. Colleagues in the team might offer alternative perspectives that enable the therapist to suspend that prejudice in order that they may be more open to the possibility of different conversations with the family. This experience is likely to create a context in which each individual within the team can further develop their self-reflexive processes.

Potential disadvantages of the team approach might include the generation of too many perspectives, making choice difficult; the clients' views become lost among the team ideas; therapists become 'reliant' on the team and their own abilities to make decisions diminish; and the power differential involved in 'more of them than there is of us'. These potential disadvantages must be reviewed constantly so that their potential is not realized, and the risk minimized. In thinking about any way of working it is important regularly to critique taken-for-granted practices so that unethical practices do not become obscured through the lens of familiarity. For example, a therapist in training who is attempting to develop the ability to maintain a particular focus in an ethically contentious area of practice, may be deflected from this development if they are offered too many choices through the medium of a reflecting team.

In particular respect to evaluating the effects of training in ethics, a useful framework for assessing the 'ethical potential' of trainee therapists is suggested by Stewart and Amundson (1995). The trainee should be able to:

- empathize sufficiently with others to imagine the consequences or potential consequences of a particular action on the other (client/trainee/colleague);

- process ethical dilemmas through using principles that guide the construction of ethical codes;
- realize that ethical codes are not an end to struggle, but that:
  - fairness,
  - justice, and
  - ethics

  are a process of struggle without a definitive end (Rorty 1991);
- reflect upon problems/tensions between and within competing values or concerns;
- carry out ethically informed decisions.

Kent (2002) of POPAN surveyed 50 UKCP training organizations on how they taught ethics. Few institutions stated specific hours of teaching, some referred to ethical teaching 'permeating' the training programme and many referred to the place of supervision as a context for developing ethical practice. Continuing professional development workshops sometimes focused specifically on ethics, but mostly ethics was included in other topics. Kent concludes that further research should aim to generate fuller responses from training institutions. She proposes that ensuring therapists learn about ethical behaviour is important and so it should have both a specific place in the curriculum and be illustrated and reinforced in supervision.

In family therapy trainings there is usually didactic teaching about both ethical principles, processes and postures, and codes of ethics: see, for example, Walrond-Skinner and Watson 1987; Inger and Inger 1994; Gergen 1994. Integration into practice through the use of live supervision, reflections during videotape review and rehearsal through role plays, is included. These methods allow for the foregrounding of circumstances in which ethical dilemmas arise, and promote the rehearsal of ethical processes, responses and attitudes.

Client groups

A wide range of clients present a variety of difficulties in both NHS and private sectors. Family therapists work with families, couples, individuals and groups. The choice of persons with whom they work may be based on a number of factors, including family preference, stage of work, geographical availability and cultural considerations.

Professionals who are significant to the family may also be included at different stages.

The term 'family' is used flexibly in the context of contemporary relationship configurations. We convene the relationship system that is regarded as significant to understanding and making a difference within the current situation. This may include family members, friends and significant professionals. The significant relationship system may vary throughout the therapy process.

The decision about who to convene is part of a process undertaken with the family. This systemic practice can access invaluable resources and needs careful negotiation of confidentiality etc. in order to minimize harmful effects. The issue of inclusion and exclusion has important ethical considerations, and therefore membership of the therapeutic system is carefully negotiated with clients through a process of relational reflexivity (Burnham 1993).

Theoretical approaches adopted by family therapists

Since its beginnings in the early 1950s, the family therapy field has used a variety of theoretical frameworks. In a linear time frame, family therapy has used psychoanalysis, cybernetics, general systems, radical constructivism, social constructionism and narrative theory. In an evolutionary sense all of these models continue to contribute to the development of the field, and each 'voice' influences the ethos of family therapists. The term 'systemic' is generally used as an umbrella term to indicate that practitioners work with human relationship systems.

Earlier approaches are now seen as operating within a 'first-order' position, in which the therapist was considered as independent of the 'observed system' which could be objectively assessed by the therapist. A 'second-order' position evolved which is more likely to consider a therapist as part of an 'observing system' (Von Foerster 1981) in which their participation in the creation of a therapeutic system is more fully considered. More recently in what has been termed the 'postmodern turn' the narrative (White and Epston 1990) and solution-focused (de Shazer 1994) models have emerged as significant approaches. Significant emphasis is on the therapist taking a 'non-expert position' from which to develop collaborative working relationships.

As the field has embraced/followed the postmodern turn, so traditional views of ethics and how to achieve an ethical practice have been challenged. The challenge to and defence of 'grand narratives' (such as the dominance of centrally determined ethical codes) is debated within the field. For example, Held (1996) and Freedman and Coombs (1996) discuss this issue from different perspectives. It seems to us that a both–and position is required here. While it is important to have a clearly defined ethical framework for a professional practice, it is also necessary to be able to exercise ethical principles in ways that produce practices that fit with local conditions. It would, however, be a mistake to think that because something is produced 'locally' it is necessarily 'good', and because something is created 'centrally' it is necessarily 'bad'.

> A family was referred for therapy in which a stepfather had sexually abused his two stepdaughters. The condition made by social services and the police for the therapy to proceed was that if any abuse more serious than was already known emerged in therapy then it should be disclosed by the therapist. The family knew of this condition and the two girls were reluctant to talk without knowing what was regarded as 'more serious'. This condition seemed to deprive the girls of the therapy they were thought to need. Renegotiations took place and the condition changed to 'any abuse that was in the past could remain in therapy, and any abuse that was current must be disclosed to social services'. This allowed the therapy to go forward and for all professionals to remain coherent within their own ethical framework. This clarity did not necessarily lead to comfort with what emerged in therapy.

The ethical practice of deconstructing taken-for-granted assumptions and practices of the 'dominant discourses' enables therapists to avoid imposing what have been called 'grand narratives' about, for example, family forms, sex stereotypes, sexual orientations and cultural practices.

This deconstructive freedom together with an intention to privilege the 'client as the expert' (Anderson and Goolishian 1992) could potentially degenerate into a situation of 'anything goes' in which a therapist cannot make decisions or influence a situation when required to. Lang *et al.* (1990) following Maturana, propose three relevant domains (production, explanation and aesthetics) for navigating ethical pathways through the day-to-day 'zones of uncertainty'

(Schön 1987; Shotter 1989). In the overarching domain of aesthetics, the professional is conscious of the ethical dimension of their practice and how they are playing out a particular moral commitment. Managing this commitment involves developing a coherent relationship between theory, practice and ethical principles. This creates a form of consciousness, promoting what is considered desirable praxis through an ethic of aspiration. For example, generating curiosity in self and others in a multiplicity of perspectives and positions; searching for meanings created in context; regarding responsibility as both personal and social; maintaining a sense of respect for the people with whom we are engaged in relation to their pains, joys, sufferings and creative potential. Production refers to a frame in which we conceive the world in the objective terms of a 'uni-verse'. Truths have been established with conventions and criteria to evaluate and make judgements about the actors and their actions in any social situation, consent is desirable but not necessary in the context of mandatory ethics. In the domain of explanation the world is conceived as a 'multi-verse' and 'the primary focus is the elaboration of many different stories and perspectives relating to the action of all participants involved in any situation' (Lang *et al.* 1990: 44). Consent is both desirable and necessary.

Practitioners are conceived as working in all domains simultaneously, though one will be foregrounded at any particular stage. For example, in situations of domestic violence, some practitioners will promote an ethic of peace by requiring an explicit commitment to non-violence before engaging in a therapeutic relationship. As part of creating an ethic of transparency, clients are informed that harm to the client or others would be an exception to the rule of confidentiality in the therapeutic relationship. During therapy, there may be times when concerns require a professional to navigate an aesthetic route between domains of production and explanation.

Other useful frameworks considering the creation of ethical practice include the coordinated management of meaning (Cronen and Pearce 1985); a model for negotiating within diversity/unity (Ravn 1991); mapping ethical process; Kitchener's model as presented in Haber (1996); relational responsibility (McNamee and Gergen 1999); creating ethical postures (Tomm 1992); and towards safe uncertainty (Mason 1993).

The theoretical affiliations of the authors could be termed 'post-Milan systemic', which is based in the original Milan approach while integrating the more recent models of narrative and solution-focused therapy.

Critical situations and their ethical resolution

Ethical technology

Beginning family therapy includes the arrangements for the working relationship, the reasons for attending, and the hoped-for outcome. Consent about working with a team via a one-way screen, and/or the use of videotape technology is an important issue. Introductions to this method of working include: reasons for its potential value, issues of use, confidentiality and storage, and reassurance that refusal will not compromise the offer of a therapeutic service. A range of options is presented for clients to consider. Consent is regularly evaluated. It may be withheld initially and given later or given at the outset and then withdrawn. Guidelines for the use of video recordings can be found in the Royal College of Psychiatrists Council Report CR79 (2000) and the Association for Family Therapy's code of ethics (2001: 17–19).

There is a growing number of ways in which technology can be used to generate options within therapy; the vignette gives just one example.

> A request was received for us to offer therapeutic work for a 13-year-old girl, on an inpatient unit, and her family. Although the girl was reluctant to attend therapy at that stage, it was hoped she would join the family for a session at some future date. The family members who attended agreed with the therapist that the girl could watch the videotape of the session with a trusted member of staff from the unit. This was to facilitate a process of 'demystifying' family therapy for the girl as well as to avoid her becoming further marginalized in a family that was undergoing profound changes in her absence. At a later stage the family used part of a session to discuss the mother/daughter relationship and how the young girl was valued and missed by her mother and the rest of the family. The experience of watching the first videotape had proved sufficiently positive for the girl to agree to watch the tape of this session with her mother.

This process helps demonstrate the many ways in which videotaping may be utilized as an integral part of a therapeutic process. Although technology has become an important aspect of systemic work in relation to forms of communication and is one of its most distinctive features, it brings its own challenges. Clearly, an argument can be made that this is an unfamiliar approach to therapy for most clients, and perhaps somewhat daunting. The power inherent in the therapeutic agency and the team itself may be seen to preclude a 'free choice' for the client: how can they refuse to become involved with this method of therapeutic work if they are not sufficiently assertive to object or if they fear they may 'lose favour'? Our wish to work with integrity within a systemic framework makes us constantly aware of these possibilities and our ethical responsibility to consider the communicative effects of the micro-practices of our everyday activity.

Who is the client? – How to begin therapy

Some families come asking for therapy as a family, whereas other families bring a particular person and present them as the problem. Some families are sent by the courts. Therapists must be able to work in a variety of circumstances. It is likely that when a family group attends an initial session they will not all be of the 'same mind', hence we are likely to ask, 'For what reason are you here today?' rather than 'What do you see as the problem?' The former can include being there because of a problem as well as reasons such as 'my wife told me to come', 'my Dad said if I didn't come then . . .', 'the school said we have to come'. In this way each person's reason for attending can be heard and respected without prejudice. People may then continue to attend for their own reasons (to help a sibling, or to be cooperative) rather than feeling they have to subscribe to the existence of a problem they do not see. When working with a group in which there are power differentials confirmed and supported by broader cultural discourses (e.g. parent/child relationship), it is important to create a context in which all voices can be heard (Hare-Mustin 1994).

Informed consent

> A family arrived having been referred by their local child and adolescent mental health service (CAMHS). The referral said that the parents had 'requested formal family therapy'. In the initial

discussions the parents said that the referrer had suggested that they 'needed formal family therapy'. Addressing this difference, the therapist said that they could not know whether the family needed family therapy or not since the therapist had not talked with them about the difficulties they were experiencing. The family members said that they were not in a position to say if they would request family therapy since they did not know enough about it. The therapist suggested that the session could end now and the family could go away and consider their options and return if they wanted. Alternatively they could continue with the current session and perhaps attend for a couple more sessions to experience the kinds of conversations that occur in family therapy. After this they could make a decision about whether they thought it might be useful to them. Thus their decision whether or not to *consent* to family therapy could be made *informed* by some knowledge of some relevant experience. In the context of such an offer this family chose to attend for two sessions and then opted into therapy.

On other occasions, clients may 'end' immediately and may or may not return later.

Working with children and adults together – power differentials in the relationship

'Do I have to come?' – autonomy/self-determination

A female-headed single-parent family with two teenage children attended for the first session. The mother showed great concern for her son and an eagerness to attend for therapy. Her son thought that he had improved sufficiently not to need therapy. How to proceed? Some team members thought that to offer/continue with therapy would 'pathologize' the boy and undermine his new-found confidence, whereas not to offer/continue therapy might undermine the concern and authority of the mother. Considerable discussion created a both–and offer. The boy's attendance was accepted as coming to 'convince' his mother that his recent changes were enduring changes, which she could support. The mother's attendance was accepted in terms of her finding ways to express her concerns, as well as

> supporting achievements. Therefore both could attend and work cooperatively together for their own 'reasons for being there'.

On other occasions, not all family members attend and some may be involved periodically as 'consultants' to the work. Convening/involving significant others may often be improved by frames such as 'partner-assisted therapy' (Asen and Jones 1999).

'Will my voice be heard?' – fairness

We wish to create ethical ways of conducting therapy in which all present are able to have a voice. Verbal skills can be weighted in favour of adult participants and can potentially disadvantage children. Creative ways of expressing ideas and feelings include the use of genograms and relationship/ecomaps, timelines, drawing, or the choice of objects to represent individuals and portray relationships. These use symbolism and metaphor to bring words into view and allow expression in ways that do not depend entirely on verbal skills, making easier access to therapy for many clients.

> A family was referred for support with reunification, the two young adult children having been removed from home and subject to care orders and multiple placements for many years. Family members experienced learning disability, and verbal communication about the concept of time, and their early collective and later individual life experiences, proved difficult. Paper was used to map out individual timelines, which converged and separated at relevant stages in their lives. This nonverbal prompt by the therapist facilitated the telling of stories, and enabled family members to ask each other questions to 'fill the gaps' in their knowledge of the others' lives, to seek clarification of events and feelings, to share emotional responses and to utilize this experience to build foundations for the new relationships that they hoped would sustain them in the next phase of their family story.

Communicating events, meanings and emotions may be expressed through physical sculpting (Burnham 1986), choreography (Papp 1984) and rituals (Imber-Black *et al.* 1988). There are numerous examples in the literature of the use of techniques such as rating scales, photographs, toys and board games, story telling, letter writing, the use of puppets, writing books with children, and so on (Wilson 1998; Freeman *et al.* 1997). The process of externalization (White 1988) separates the person from the problem, decreases the oppressive influence of problems, increases a sense of personal agency and can be achieved both linguistically and actively. Reflexive future orientations (Boscolo *et al.* 1987), solution-focused practice (de Shazer 1994), reflecting processes (Andersen 1995) and appreciative inquiry (Cooperrider and Srivasta 1987) stand alongside narrative therapy as approaches that actively empower both adult and child clients towards preferred futures.

Confidentiality

Confidentiality is both a decision and an ongoing process. When the membership of the therapeutic system changes during the course of therapy, then confidentiality may be negotiated and renegotiated. For example, in an inpatient unit with many professionals involved in the care and therapy of the resident, it is important to create 'joined up' professional relationships to construct an ethically coherent service. Confidentiality in this context would include the ethical exchange of information between professionals. When this works well, many families appreciate the coordination of the service they experience. At times, and in specific circumstances, this general confidentiality will need to be renegotiated. Some clients may request that the content of family therapy sessions not be made generally available to the ward staff. In both child and adult services this can be specifically negotiated within the contexts of both mandatory ethics and aspirational ethics. This embargo may be time specific and part of the therapeutic process, and an outcome may be the facilitation of the client's being able to discuss the issues with the ward staff in, and with, greater 'confidence'.

Whether to include children in sessions when discussing adult issues will be influenced by both the cultural values of the therapist and the ethic of protecting children from harm or potential harm. For example, when a topic related to the relationship between adults is raised as significant to the therapy, it can be difficult to decide whether to continue to include the children in further conversation. Involving the children in issues such as domestic violence and marital disharmony may be thought to harm the children and distress the adults. On the other hand, if the children are already witness to, and participants in, the episodes, then how will their voices and experience be heard? In this dilemma, inquiries are made about how much the children are aware of or are involved in the episodes. If they are significantly involved then they usually stay until such time as it is useful or desirable for them to leave. Children have said that they are glad to have stayed since they feel that their opinions have been listened to and may have had an influence in creating a more positive future.

When children and significant others are not able to be included in a session then methods such as 'internalized other interviewing' (Tomm 1994; Epston 1993; Burnham 2000) are useful to achieve inclusive interviewing.

Innovative ways of generating interpersonal resources include changing the membership of sessions. For example, multiple family therapy (Asen 2002), inpatient units and family–professional meetings.

Within the room, family members do not always want to say what is on their minds in the presence of other family members. Family therapists have developed ways to facilitate a conversation that has therapeutic potential with everyone in the room or may see family members separately and then reconvene. Making the distinction between content and process can be helpful to work on an issue whilst maintaining confidentiality.

> A young man was referred when it came to the notice of his GP (via his parents) that he was 'cross-dressing'. The whole family was invited to a first meeting. When exploring the matter of concern, the parent said that his siblings (older brother and younger sister), did not know of the cause for concern. The therapist asked the boy if he would be prepared for his siblings to know about the issue if the therapist thought it was necessary. The boy said that he would prefer them not to know but agreed if the therapist thought it necessary. The therapist explored the situation using process-oriented questions around personal and interpersonal relationships, without naming the content (cross-dressing). The siblings agreed to make changes without knowing why, only that it might make their brother feel better. The therapy proceeded successfully, involving the other family members as a resource, without ever naming the issue of concern.

This approach can be useful in a range of situations (including those in which children are present in a session when discussing violence between the parents or the couple's relationship).

Confidentiality is also an issue outside the room. Family members may call or write to the therapist between sessions and wish to impart information about themselves or another member of the family. This situation needs to be handled respectfully without creating 'secrets', which would inhibit the therapeutic process. For example, when someone rings between sessions it can be useful to ask politely if they can delay saying what they have rung about until they have been asked some questions. The therapist may then proceed with questions such as: 'Do the other people know that you have rung?', 'How will they learn about this call?', 'How would it be if you talked about this in the next session?', 'How will it help for me to listen to this information?' The outcome may be that the person: decides not to continue the conversation and to raise the issue in the next session; has already made an agreement with the family to make the call; is willing to openly discuss the call in the next session. It may be that the call is in the 'domain of production' and requires action on the part of the therapist in relation to its content.

Moving between whole family sessions and individual sessions

Ethical principles need to consider how to enable the therapist to meet with family 'sub-systems', for example parents or sibling groups, and then to move back to the whole family while maintaining a relationship that has therapeutic potential for all members.

Cultural beliefs and practices

As societies become more cosmopolitan, therapists and therapy need to develop a more flexible approach to the families they meet. Therapists can use ethical principles to guide them in how to work with families who are from a different culture from themselves, who are made up of members from different cultures, and those in which different family members have a different relationship with the 'host' culture.

> A family consisted of mother and father (who came to England from Asia) and their daughter (15) and son (14), both born in

the UK. In a clear and unambiguous way, the son was given individual responsibility for distressing the family. Within the family, the father maintained the values of traditional Asian parenting, while the mother integrated some parenting practices influenced by the 'host' culture. The children were, for a considerable part of their lives, living in a westernized way. Using an ethic of 'relational responsibility', the team reflected in the presence of therapist and family, offering ideas about how intergenerational differences and being part of different cultures influenced ways of living. Each member of the family was able to recognize this as a major influence on the difficulties that they were experiencing. Family members began to consider difficulties experienced within the family from a relational perspective as well as individual. McNamee and Gergen (1999): 'We hold relationally responsible actions to be those that sustain and enhance forms of interchange out of which meaningful action itself is made possible.'

Emergent issues

With the advent of family therapy in the field of psychotherapy it is not always possible to be clear about who the client is, and so the ethics of justice (based on individual rights) are not always adequate. An ethic of care is also necessary, which takes into account the relational context in which ethical practices are made.

In the context of recent research by Newfield *et al.* (2000), Hoffman (2002) explores the relationship between the ethic of justice (followed by professional organizations) and the ethic of care (followed by family therapists). Newfield *et al.* researched ethical decision making among family therapists and individual therapists. To do this, they identified two well-known conceptual camps. One was the justice model of moral reasoning developed by Kohlberg (1981), based on the rights and obligations of the individual and emphasizing abstract principles of fairness, equality and what is right. The other was the ethic of care model put forward by Gilligan (1982), which embeds moral decisions in relational contexts, and for this reason their possible impact on the relational field must be carefully considered. The authors concluded that the ethical guidelines, which now exist, should be modified to include a relational ethic. In their words:

> Guidance for considering relationship responsibilities [should] be modified by the addition of a relationship-caring process . . . [which addresses] the relationship complexities consistently identified by therapists as ethically challenging.
>
> (Newfield *et al.* 2000: 185)

The requirement for such changes is perhaps indicated by the challenges presented to family therapists (and others) by the ever-changing nature of the family and other significant relational systems. The number of family forms created by 'non-traditional methods', same-sex relationships and cross-cultural marriages means that therapists are likely to need to extend their relational thinking beyond what they currently know in order to work towards the best interests of those who seek their help.

In conclusion, family therapy is accepted as a valuable form of practice across a wide range of agencies. Research findings support its efficacy, and its use is becoming more widespread. Professionals in health and social care are frequently introduced to this way of working within their initial training and can choose to train towards qualification as a registered practitioner. The UKCP is clarifying standards of practice and training, and the prospect of statutory regulation exists. In an increasingly cosmopolitan and changing world, the ways in which family relationships are created and re-created require therapists to be vigilant about the effects of values and principles that have guided their intentions and actions thus far. Mandatory ethics are essential to give clear direction in uncertain or ambiguous circumstances. Therapists, both individually and collectively, must always aspire to improve practice towards the co-creation of what is in the best interests of all in newly emerging contexts for clients themselves, culture and society.

References

Andersen, T. (1995) Reflecting processes. Acts of informing and forming: You can borrow my eyes but you must not take them away from me!, in S. Friedman (ed.) *The Reflecting Team in Action: Collaborative Practice in Family Therapy*. New York: Guilford Press.

Anderson, H. and Goolishian, H. (1992) The client is the expert: a not-knowing approach to therapy, in S. McNamee and K.J. Gergen (eds) *Therapy as Social Construction*. London: Sage.

Asen, E. (2002) Multiple family therapy: an overview, *Journal of Family Therapy* 24: 3–16.

Asen, E. and Jones, E. (1999) Systemic therapy for depression, *Context*, 41 (February): 22–3.

Association for Family Therapy (1999) *The Blue Book*. AFT Publishing.

Association for Family Therapy (2001) Code of ethics, *Context*, 53 (February): 41–3.

Austin, K.M., Molien, M.E. and Williams, G.T. (1990) *Confronting Malpractice: Legal and Ethical Dilemmas in Psychotherapy*. London: Sage.

Boscolo, L., Cecchin, G., Hoffman, L. *et al.* (1987) *Milan Systemic Family Therapy: Conversations in Theory and Practice*. New York: Basic Books.

Burnham, J. (1986) *Family Therapy: First Steps Towards* a *Systemic Approach*. London: Tavistock.

Burnham, J. (1993) *Voices from the Training Context*, special edition of *Human Systems*, 4(3–4).

Burnham, J. (2000) Internalised other interviewing: evaluating and enhancing empathy, *Clinical Psychology Forum. Vol. 140. Working with Adults and Children*. Leicester: British Psychological Society.

Carr, A. (2000a) Evidence-based practice in family therapy and systemic consultation. I: Child-focused problems, *Journal of Family Therapy*, 22: 29–60.

Carr, A. (2000b) Evidence-based practice in family therapy and systemic consultation. II: Adult-focused problems, *Journal of Family Therapy*, 22: 273–95.

Cooperrider, D.L. and Srivasta, S. (1987) Appreciative Inquiry in Organisational Life, *Research in Organisational Change and Development*, 1: 129–69.

Crane, R.D. and Hafen Jr, M. (2002) Meeting the needs of evidenced-based practice in family therapy: developing the scientist–practitioner model, *Journal of Family Therapy* 24(2): 113–24.

Cronen, V.E. and Pearce, W.B. (1985) Toward an explanation of how the Milan method works: an invitation to a systemic epistemology and the evolution of family systems, in D. Campbell and R. Draper (eds) *Applications of Systemic Therapy: The Milan Approach*. London: Grune & Stratton.

de Shazer S. (1994) *Words were Originally Magic*. New York: Norton.

Epston, D. (1993) Internalising discourses versus externalising discourses, in S. Gilligan and R. Price (eds) *Therapeutic Conversations*. London: Norton.

Freedman, J. and Coombs, G. (1996) Relationships and ethics, in *Narrative Therapy: The Social Construction of Preferred Realities*. London: Norton.

Freeman, J., Epston, D. and Lobovits, D. (1997) *Playful Approaches to Serious Problems: Narrative Therapy with Children and their Families*. London: Norton.

Gergen, K.G. (1994) *Realities and Relationships: Soundings in Social Construction*. Cambridge, MA: Harvard Publications.

Gilligan, C. (1982) *In a Different Voice*. Cambridge, MA: Harvard University Press.

Haber, R. (1996) *Dimensions of Psychotherapy Supervision: Maps and Means*. London: Norton.

Hare-Mustin, R.T. (1994) Discourses in the mirrored room: a postmodern analysis of therapy, *Family Process*, 33: 19–35.

Held, B.S. (1996) Ethical and other practical implications of postmodern antirealism in therapy, in B.S. Held (ed.) *Back to Reality: A Critique of Postmodern Theory in Psychotherapy*. London: Norton.

Hoffman, L., (1981) *Foundations of Family Therapy*. New York. Basic Books.

Hoffman L. (2002) *Family Therapy: An Intimate History*. London: Norton.

Hubble, M.A., Duncan, B.L. and Miller S.D. (1999) *The Heart and Soul of Change: What Works in Therapy*. Washington, DC: American Psychological Association.

Imber-Black, E., Roberts, J. and Whiting, R. (1988) *Rituals in Families and Family Therapy*. London: Norton.

Inger, I.B. and Inger, J. (1994) *Creating an Ethical Position in Family Therapy*. London: Karnac.

Kent, R. (2002) Ethical practice and psychotherapy training, *The Psychotherapist*. 19: 34–6.

Kohlberg, L. (1981) *The Philosophy of Moral Development*. San Francisco: Harper & Row.

Lang, W.P., Little, M. and Cronen, V. (1990) The systemic professional: domains of action and the question of neutrality, *Human Systems*, 1: 1.

Mason, B. (1993) Towards positions of safe uncertainty, *Voices from the Training Context*, special edition of *Human Systems*, 4(3–4).

McNamee, S. and Gergen, K. (1999) *Relational Responsibility: Resources for Sustainable Dialogue*. London: Sage.

Newfield, S., Newfield, H., Sperry, J. *et al.* (2000) Ethical decision-making among family therapists and individual therapists, *Family Process*, 39: 177–88.

Papp, P. (1984) *The Process of Change*. New York: Gardner Press.

Ravn, I. (1991) What should guide reality construction?, in F. Stier (ed.) *Research and Reflexivity*. London: Sage.

Rorty, R. (1991) Objectivity, relativism, and truth, *Philosophical Papers*, Vol. 1. New York: Cambridge University Press.

Royal College of Psychiatrists (2000) *Council Report*, CR79.

Schön, D.A. (1987) *Educating the Reflective Practitioner*. San Francisco: Jossey-Bass.

Shotter, J. (1989) Social accountability and the social construction of you, in J. Shotter and K.J. Gergen (eds) *Texts of Identity*. London: Sage.

Stewart, K. and Amundson, J. (1995) The ethical postmodernist: or not everything is relative all at once, *Journal of Systemic Therapies*, 14(2): 70–8.

Tomm, K. (1992) Ethical postures in therapy, *Context*, 11 (Summer): 12–13.

Tomm, K. (1994) Internalised other interviewing: a sequence for couple work. Workshop paper.

Von Foerster, H. (1981) On constructing a reality, *Observing Systems*. Seaside, CA: Intersystems.

Walrond-Skinner, S. and Watson, D. (1987) *Ethical Issues in Family Therapy*. London: Routledge & Kegan Paul.

Wilson, J. (1998) *Child Focused Practice*: A *Collaborative Systemic Approach*. London: Karnac.

White, M. (1988) Externalising the problem, *Dulwich Centre Newsletter*.

White, M. and Epston, D. (1990) *Narrative Means to Therapeutic Ends*. New York: Norton.

8 Ethical issues in group therapy

Mark Aveline

Characteristics of group therapy

In contrast to individual therapy, groups offer a rich opportunity for interaction with several others, each of whose experience of life and style of coping with 'problems-in-living' are different. Where one group member may be weak, another will be strong. Where one may be beginning, another may be some way down a path of similar personal difficulty and can offer guidance and assistance with unfamiliar terrain. Beneficially, these roles are not fixed and may alternate within sessions and over time. Groups offer the opportunity to be altruistic and discover that one can be of assistance to others, with all that that implies for improving an inner sense of worthlessness. Being a member of a cohesive, purposeful group may be a uniquely encouraging experience in a person's life. No other therapy offers such opportunities for interpersonal learning. Members can test out how they are seen, experience how their inner selves are received and, most importantly, come to know which aspects of themselves may be valued by their peers. Individuals can be faced with the effects that problematic, maladaptive interpersonal acts have on others, and have the opportunity to, first, recognize and, then, modify defensive self-limiting strategies. The reactions of fellow members – challenging, discriminating, applauding, sceptical – have great force, because they are seen as coming from unbiased peers and not from therapists who are compelled, professionally or financially, to be supportive. In a stranger therapy group, members can take risks; they can try out interactions that might be too hazardous, shameful or simply unacceptable in the natural social groups of family, friends and work where others have their own agendas and limiting expectations.

Group therapy has enormous potential to influence its members, but, like all forces, this may be for the worse rather than for the better. In the group, members are themselves; they do more than talk about their problems: they demonstrate their problems in relationship. This may be uncomfortable or discouraging for other members. Furthermore, how one person is may accentuate the conflicts and inner doubts of another (negative fit). Unhelpful collective processes may seize the group when, for example, individuals are demonized (scapegoated) and extruded, or there is collusion with unhealthy patterns (pairing, idealization and false solutions), or, simply, a general negativity and apathy develops (Foulkes and Anthony 1957; Bion 1961; Whitaker 1985). Groups can be poorly led. Leaders may be deficient in vision of what can be achieved or, worse, narcissistic or exploitative in character. As a couple, leaders can be dysfunctional.

Groups are powerful organizations, deeply shaped by their history, and hard for individuals to resist. They quickly establish their own culture, which is wonderful when it is therapeutic but obviously not when apathy and toxicity is the rule. Group therapy is intrinsically a complex therapy, requiring the leaders to be competent in understanding group and individual process and having the ability to make decisions, which balance the needs of individual members and the *group-as-a-whole* (Aveline 1988). Often, making these decisions is uncomfortable, especially when the therapist is forced to favour one need over another; these decisions should be ethically informed.

My context, group therapy assumptions and ethical frame

In May 2002, I retired after 27 years in post as a consultant medical psychotherapist in Nottingham. The Nottingham Psychotherapy Unit provides a 'one-stop' integrated specialist service in psychodynamic and cognitive-behavioural psychotherapy. As a tertiary NHS facility, it receives referrals of patients whose problems are too complex or time consuming to be treated in primary or secondary healthcare. This means that, for the most part, patient problems are recurrent and ingrained. While the presenting symptoms vary in form, the fundamental problem of the majority seen in the psychodynamic division is in relationships.

Group therapy is the therapy of choice for nearly a half of those offered dynamic psychotherapy. Open and closed groups are provided; some have a special focus, such as women who have been sexually abused in childhood. My own interest was in weekly therapy groups, meeting for 90-minute sessions. These were slow open groups, topping up with new members as established members graduated or left. Most patients stayed in the group for 18 months, with a minimum commitment of 6 months and a maximum membership of 2 years. Generally, I worked with a co-leader, preferably a woman so as to balance my male presence. I also had a particular interest in closed brief training groups for healthcare professionals (Aveline 1986a,b, 1992). The currency of these groups is words, although action techniques may also be used (Aveline 1979).

My orientation is interpersonal (Ratigan and Aveline 1988; Aveline 1990; Yalom 1995). In the here-and-now of the group, members manifest their interpersonal problems in their interaction with their peers and with the leaders. Collectively and individually, everyone has the opportunity to work on the problems. The group is a social microcosm. It is ahistorical, not requiring deep knowledge of the person's history to be effective; it can work with biography in the making. The experience of social cohesion and interpersonal learning through disclosure, feedback and process reflection on what is happening within the group (reflective loop) are key therapeutic factors. The group relies on trust, honesty and hard work. Its success depends on the members' generosity and altruism: rich gifts with the potential to transform recipients; painfully missed when they are absent.

My work has to be ethical; many official bodies regulate it. As a doctor, the General Medical Council governs me, and as a psychiatrist the Royal College of Psychiatrists. While I maintained my registration with UKCP, I was answerable to them. Now I have a similar position with BACP whose ethical principles of fidelity, autonomy, beneficence, non-maleficence, justice and self-respect are succinct and apposite (BACP 2002). Each body has its ethical code, which, like good law, aims to codify what is fair and good practice. However, external regulation is a weak constraint compared with the therapist's internalized ethic, the personal, private undertaking that is made in every therapy. The Psychotherapy and Counselling Oath is one attempt to voice what we judged personally to be important (Aveline and Clarkson 1997).

Put simply, my personal ethical code enjoins me to:

- uphold good practice and, as far as possible, be effective in what I do;
- act in the patient's best interest (patients are people who suffer and whom I am trying to help);
- refrain from all intentional ill-doing;
- not do harm;
- recognize my duty of care to others as well as to the patient;
- help the patient make informed choices and take responsibility for what they are responsible for in their life;
- be modest about my knowledge and ability;
- act in good faith, not abusing my privileged position of power and access to confidences;
- be truthful, but tactfully;
- be tolerant and show humility, respecting the decisions of my patients and the struggles that they have had in their lives and the compromises that they have had to make;
- take care of my health and that of my colleagues and family. While my own discomfort comes a long way behind my patient's in priority, I am of no use to that person if I do not survive.

In short, take good care.

In group therapy, a general ethical stance is necessary – just as much as in any form of therapy – but special problems arise from the method itself. My primary aim is to facilitate members to be therapeutic for each other. The more I can be in the background, the better. To a significant degree, I see myself as a fellow traveller, rather than all-competent, all-knowing leader. But my position is not one of abdication. Within the limits of my capacity to influence, I have responsibility for the good functioning of the group. I hold the boundaries of the group and have ultimate say on who joins and leaves and when. I have to strike a balance between upholding the rights of the individual to be themselves within the group and the greatest good for the group as a whole. The balance is not either/or but a fluctuating compensation for what my co-leader and I see as antitherapeutic processes. Often, leaders have to act on both sides of the balance.

Guiding principles in group therapy

The following are questions I ask myself:

- Whose benefit has priority?
- Whose interests do I have in mind? What consequences follow?
    - Group member
    - Group as a whole
    - My reputation as a therapist
    - My comfort as a therapist in the group
    - My own voyeuristic satisfaction
    - Rivalry, collaboration or intimacy with my co-leader
    - Clinical service priorities, for example to have so many groups of particular durations running.
- What parameters can help my clinical decision?
    - Appropriateness of particular group for specific problems
    - Stage of group
    - Stage of members
    - Capacity and readiness of individual members for mature action
    - Competence and willingness of the group to address and resolve the issue
    - Competence and confidence of leaders
    - External containment, for example supervision, clinical service structure, violence management
    - How well the issue has been addressed (accuracy, intelligibly, over sufficient period).

Types of intervention

To influence the group, I have various types of intervention of escalating force (listed below). In some, I am the primary actor; in others the responsibility lies with the group to act. In all cases, I have to be sure that I am acting ethically.

1. By dictate or discussion, establish enabling ground rules.
2. Trust the group to resolve the problem and, therefore, wait

for that to happen. But for how long, and judged by what outcome?

3. Identify the problem to the group.
4. Analyse the problem by interpretation.
5. Draw attention to process.
6. Encourage group discussion and resolution.
7. Wait.
8. Repeat 1 to 7, again and again.
9. Model healthy address
10. Assert/enforce ground rules and healthy address by:
    (a) interrupting;
    (b) changing topic;
    (c) breaking up harmful patterns (for the group and for individuals), for example monopolizing, having nothing to say and being on the sidelines. But striving always to be aware of what members can bear emotionally and how ready they are to take the next step;
    (d) Issuing an ultimatum;
    (e) Eject member(s);
    (f) Suspend/close group.

Critical situations and their ethical resolution

Ethics cannot be compartmentalized into neat, separate areas. The principles feed one into another and contribute in varying degree to each situation.

Selection and retention

When a practitioner has only one form of intervention to offer to someone seeking help, the pragmatic question is: is this therapy relevant, appropriate and sufficiently safe for this patient? The ethical question is one of quality. Do I as practitioner have confidence that what I am offering is good practice? (See section on competence). Should I know that this is not the case and I persist in my offer, I would be abusing my position of power, which stems from my expert knowledge of the proposed group and the nature of the patient's problems. I must honour the trust placed in me (fidelity).

When a range of therapies is on offer, additional issues arise. The practitioner has to ask themself whose interest they have in mind. On economic or ideological grounds, a clinical service may be under pressure to direct a set proportion of patients to group therapy. The viability of a particular group may be at risk through dwindling membership or the need to continue a group to a particular time-point. Subtle and not so subtle pressures subvert the practitioner's ethical focus on the patient's need and make it easy to rationalize questionable decisions. When several group members share a relationship style, the group can get stuck in one unhelpful way of seeing things. A new member with a different, more enabling way of perceiving the world can seem like a godsend for the desperate therapist. It might be clinically right for that person to join the group but it would not be acting in their best interest to recruit them for the group's salvation alone. Similarly, a patient who is very handicapped emotionally would not be well served by joining a group that is functioning at a high level of maturity.

Ending

Issues around ending can be ethically challenging.

> Sarah had done well in a slow open group. Over 18 months, she had become confident in expressing her opinion. Timidity and anxious deference had given way to a much more assertive and attractive persona. She was an excellent role model for the group, embodying hope for new members and able to think psychologically about individual and group process. The leaders decided to end the group in a year's time, thus exceeding the upper limit of two years for Sarah's membership. She was offered and accepted an extension to the end of the group but, within a couple of months, changed her mind and left the group. This was the right decision for her but a blow for the group and leaders alike. The temptation to try to press her to stay was great. Putting forward spurious reasons for her to continue in the group, for example to consolidate her gain or confront her avoidance of ending, were manifestations of *our* loss and anger at being abandoned. Ethically, we had to let her go and work through our less than generous reactions. The alert came in the form of a sequence of feelings. A guilty sense of knowing what one ought to do being temporarily submerged

> by ever so positive seductive rationalizations to do the opposite. For a while, the answer to the question 'Whose interests do I have in mind?' was all too plain. Sarah's autonomy was at risk.

Transparency is one way to guard against temptation. For most patients, group therapy will be unfamiliar territory. It is important to help the prospective member make an informed judgement about joining a particular group. In my practice that involved one or two preparatory meetings, describing what happens in groups in general and this group in particular, going through written ground rules, which set out mutual expectations and optimum participation, and anticipating the likely problematic interpersonal processes that will be engaged in the patient and which may lead to premature dropout. I would review candidly the possible benefit from membership and the hard work that would be necessary. For some years, I supplemented this by having the prospective member view a 30-minute preparatory film that I had made about a real group and a meeting with the members of the proposed group. 'Don't oversell' and 'Promote informed consent' were my mottos. When I did not follow these precepts, I knew that I was on the slippery slope of ethical compromise.

Capacity

Capacity to cope successfully with impasses within the group is a function of both individual members and the collective of the group as a whole.

Maladaptive patterns of relationship and thinking are maintained by repetition; people fall back on tried and tested ways of getting by instead of trying something new. The group may do the same, for example when members take flight into social chitchat in order to avoid risking putting forward their own agendas for exploration. The consequence is a trade of self-limitation for safety; the trade may be done consciously or unconsciously. Therapy, however, disrupts these life-solutions by tipping the balance away from the comfort of safety towards new ways of living, which characteristically are viewed initially with trepidation. Doing what is personally difficult lies at the heart of successful therapy. The way to make progress is not to stay in the safe zone.

Good morale in group therapy is sustained by members taking risks and making progress. It is all too easy for the group or the leader(s) to become impatient and demand a rate of progress that is too much for members. What is too much for particular members is not fixed. Subtle processes operate. Generally the group rewards disclosure and self-reflection with approval and, hence, encourages more of the same. However, reasonably or not, the individual may suddenly feel exposed and then want and need to rein back, much to the group's disappointment. The group may react by increasing pressure, for example to disclose, participate more or change. On the other hand, a mature *working* group will be able to change direction and accommodate what may be justified caution on the part of the member by backing off or exploring the individual's dynamic of need for safety or the group's dynamic of need for progress.

Ethical issues concern the balance between the individual right to safety and the group's right to function in a way that enables change. In the following vignettes, Jane had capacity (just) to cope with impasses whereas Sandra did not.

> Jane came from a strict religious home where the children were frequently punished; the atmosphere was austere and needs were denied. Jane's way of surviving was to comply obsessionally. Her compliance concealed a deep well of angry resentment with authority figures. Sadly, she resembled her parents in being critical and quick to find fault in others.
>
> In the group, she spoke repeatedly of the malign incompetence of her managers at work. Ever since the fault-finding conclusion of a complaints procedure four years before, they could do nothing right in her eyes. Experiencing the discomfort of her unending and zealous criticism, the group had an insight into her contribution to the situation. Jane, however, could not accept that she could be alienating and intimidating (blind spot) and felt so attacked and persecuted by the group when the alternative view was pressed that she was ready to leave. The group was right to press her, as her way of interacting was central to her problem but her capacity to consider the insight was limited; the belief was too central to her view of the world to be jettisoned. We as leaders judged that she was at risk of harm and acted to minimize maleficence by diverting the group from a path that was going nowhere. We encouraged members to reflect on what the frustration with Jane meant in terms of their

own dynamics and asked whom else in the group wanted time for their issues.

The group had more success in exploring her starkly different relationship with two young men in the group. Though both were out of work and underachieving, with one she was patient and forgiving and with the other, fierce in criticizing his indolence and conceit. With the first young man she was a loving mother, albeit somewhat overprotective. This paralleled her good relationship with her daughter, of which she was proud and for which the group praised her. The second young man appeared to represent an unacceptable part of herself that she attacked with all the ferocity of her parents. Because her mothering role was positive, she was able to tolerate some exploration.

Sandra's capacity was even more limited. Severely sexually abused in childhood, her adult life was chaotic. It was impossible for her to maintain a constant view of others. She alternated between dependence and hate-filled attack. She monopolized time in the group, working herself into terrifying rages, and causing the leaders to fear for their safety. Following discussion with the supervisor, a colleague volunteered to stand outside the group room door when the leaders judged that the risk of violence was high (self-respect). This helped contain the situation.

Threat of self-harm

David, a group member, becomes distressed. Despite entreaties to stay, he runs out of the room. Members are left feeling upset and fearful that he will injure himself. What does the group do? Do some or all go after him, or do they stay and process what has happened? The leaders and the group (by virtue of the form of therapy) have some responsibility for David's welfare but there is also responsibility for the group and the other members.

Going after David means that his state is given priority over others' and that the rest of the group will have less time for themselves (risk of injustice). Sometimes this is inevitable if the risk of significant self-harm is high. Generally in group therapy, the ethical stance would be that David is a responsible human being and has autonomy to leave the session prematurely. He and the group would know that the group meets within definite parameters of place and time and is available as a forum in which to work on pressing problems. Members chose to engage or not. This stance risks harm to David but gives precedence to justice for the others and respects his autonomy; everyone has to live with the anxiety of possibly having made a mistake.

Ejection

Terminating a patient's membership of a group or, even, the group itself is a drastic, rare step. Certain acts, if not resolved, ultimately sabotage the group and the member's chance of benefit. But with my interpersonal focus on the patient's problems-in-living, I welcome the person embodying their problem. Persons being themselves with all the interactional discomforts that follow is meat and drink for the group. The key therapeutic point is: can the person pull back from simply being to reflecting on their way of being, to recognizing and owning feelings and behaviour, and working on their modification? This is always difficult to do. Sometimes, it is beyond the member's capacity and their behaviour is so extreme that they threaten to destroy the group.

> Miranda, pretty and vivacious, made a big impact when she joined the group. Her magnetism and zest for life attracted everyone. Each week, there was a new graphic episode in her life story: abusive jealous ex-partners, cruel unthinking officials, an empty larder. Her young children were little more than ghostly presences in the stories. The group swung into action, eagerly soliciting the latest developments, being outraged and offering solutions. She drew out other members, especially the men but, somehow, while the focus might start with them, it soon returned to her. There were hints that she was meeting with members outside the session, a breach of the ground rules. One male member, John, adored her and the group applauded their relationship. She habitually came late to the sessions. Despite our efforts as leaders, the group did not effectively start until she arrived. She would take the chair next to me, dressed in eye-catching clothes, and be charming. It was difficult not to be caught up in the fascination. The restraining tug of my co-leader reined in lust and spurred on analysis.
>
> There was lots of energy in the group but, instead of being

> evenly shared out, it was being directed to one person, Miranda. She could not see that there was any problem with the pattern. Worse still, neither could the group. When we interpreted the process (pairing, idealization, splitting and projection), the group reacted with hostility, equating us with the cruel officials that persecuted Miranda and being jealous of the half-declared affair with John. While they would take to task other members who arrived late, Miranda was excused. The group was not working. No therapy was being done. Ultimata were ignored. The climax came when most members went to an all-night party at Miranda's house. The children were reported to be lying neglected while the party raged. A fight broke out.
>
> There was nothing left in our therapy armamentarium but to terminate Miranda's membership of the group; we had run through the interventions listed earlier. John left too and moved in with Miranda. The relationship became explosive and violent, another sad repetition in Miranda's history; the household was overwhelmed with debt and the children taken into care. The group, itself, nearly foundered. Our reputation as caring therapists was savaged.
>
> Miranda's capacity for reflection and work in therapy was very limited. Arguably, it was so limited that she should not have been offered therapy at all. On the other hand, the group offered her the opportunity to learn about her patterns of interaction and their significance, and make changes in the here-and-now. Ethically, we had a duty of care to her but, at the end, we had a larger duty of care to the rest of the group. Once that became plain, we had to act to secure the greatest good (justice) for the majority.

This is a dramatic example but, at a lesser level, balancing the wishes/needs of one member over another and the group as a whole is an everyday part of group leadership. For example, monopolizing is a familiar issue. A member likes to talk and wants to talk; others who fear being in the spotlight collude with the preference. Acts by the leader such as interrupting the talker, redirecting the conversation, and interpreting the pattern, all prioritize others and are ethically correct. The leader has a duty of care to all and not just to the fascinating or monopolizing one. Conversely, when the group scapegoats, the duty may be to protect the one from the many.

Confidentiality

Group reports written by the leaders and circulated to members are a common way of enhancing the effect of the session (Yalom *et al.* 1975; Aveline 1986b). The ethical problem is confidentiality. All therapy groups operate with the ground rule that what happens within the group is confidential. Members vary in how much they say about sessions to partners or family. Group reports raise the stakes as there is a record that can be read by anyone. Of course, only first names are used in the report, but many details of interaction and sometimes of history are recorded. The leaders' ethical duty to promote well-being is dependent on the group's actions as well as their own. The issue of confidentiality must be addressed in the group. A common resolution is for members to speak outside only of their interactions and for them to stress that perspective and confidentiality to any outside person.

A similar issue arises when someone has not attended the group for several weeks. At what point should they no longer receive the group report? Membership and access to each other's stories is earned through attendance and joint commitment to the principles of the group.

Competence

In a classic study by Yalom and Lieberman (1971), dysfunctional patterns were identified in encounter group leaders. It concluded that individuals in groups led by the charismatic, narcissistic and excessively confrontative were at risk of harm whereas those leaders who operated in the mid-range of confrontation and were high in caring and meaning attribution had much better outcomes. In my view, it is preferable for groups to be co-led, though this is not a guarantee of beneficence.

Usually it will be the supervisor that identifies problems between leaders that might be to the detriment of the group and may have a duty to act to prevent harm and to ensure provision of good service.

> Carol and Roger co-lead a group. After a while, colleagues realized that they were having an affair. Later their relationship deteriorated and both became erratic in their behaviour. This

> could not be adequately addressed in supervision and, indeed, attempts to do so were resented as an unwarranted intrusion. Eventually, the supervisor had to rule that the group could not continue.

Intimate relationships between co-leaders are not necessarily harmful to the group, but there is a risk that they will take priority over the group and that members will be drawn into acting out conflicts that are not theirs.

Emergent issues

User perspectives on therapy and evaluation of outcomes

One of the consistent trends in psychotherapy research is for therapists to overestimate the effect of the therapy and to differ from clients in their perception of what is important in sessions. While accepting the point that what is seen to be important may not be that important in catalysing change, all perceptions are valuable and need to be considered.

Within the NHS, great emphasis is now placed on the consumer perspective. This has the potential to redesign the way that therapy is delivered, both in the practical arrangements to do with access and in secondary support, for example crèches and the therapy itself. The ethical purposes of beneficence and respecting autonomy would be served by taking consumer views seriously.

Power and responsibility in the therapeutic community

The therapeutic community (TC) is the most radical counter to the power inequality of the therapy relationship. Grounded in the principles of democratization, permissiveness, reality-confrontation and communalism (Rapaport 1960), power is shared equally between patients and staff, extreme behaviour is tolerated while at the same time members are confronted with the effects of their actions, all within the context of a close community that provides a living-learning experience. The approach emphasizes patient autonomy but could jeopardize justice for some.

Residents (patients) have substantial responsibility for admission and discharge from the TC. Admission depends on fellow patient support for the decision. There is much to be said for this, as members know the psychological problems from inside and can see when someone is working or not. But here is one of the ethical dilemmas of group therapy. The work depends on members making fair decisions; except in extreme circumstances, the therapists have one voice among many. Therapists have to trust the group to have integrity and wisdom; this can be a nerve-racking process. Inevitably, mistakes will be made, especially when a collective process to split and scapegoat seizes the TC or group. How far can the staff let the process go? When do they have to intervene to protect the one from the many or, conversely, the many from the one when the one is exploiting the TC rules to the detriment of others?

Giving voice to the muted

When, as now in the UK, there is insufficient provision of acute psychiatric beds, only those in desperate straits can gain admission. Admission is a major life event, signifying that that person cannot at that moment manage their life. Roles that in everyday life sustain identity and worth are lost, albeit with good fortune only temporarily. Ward practice is biased towards the management of severe mental disorder, largely through drug therapy and safety-first risk reduction. In this disturbed and pressured environment, the patient's voice as a rounded, potentially competent human being is muted. Group therapy in the form of ward meetings can be a force for good and ethically asserts patients' autonomy. Voicing experience of what brought people to admission, their reactions to ward life, and sharing recovery and setback, bring the person to the fore (beneficence). Patients and staff see each other in new, less impoverished ways. Sadly, this rosy scenario is fading, rather than emergent. Group therapy skills are lacking and many clinicians lack confidence in the method.

Conclusion

What happens in a therapy group is the product of all the participants. While groups have considerable capacity for self-healing, collective processes or persons acting destructively (including the leaders) can wreck the good functioning of the group and damage its therapeutic potential. For the leaders, judging what is likely to happen and facing up to what has to be done often poses uncomfortable choices in which the needs and wishes of one party have to be subordinated to another's. Ethical consideration brings the conflict into focus and points to the path that ought to be followed, which is not the one of seductive rationalization.

References

Aveline, M. (1979) Action techniques in psychotherapy, *British Journal of Hospital Medicine*, 22: 78–84.

Aveline, M. (1986a) Personal themes from training groups for health care professionals, *British Journal of Medical Psychology*, 59: 325–35.

Aveline, M. (1986b) The use of written reports in a brief group psychotherapy, *International Journal of Group Psychotherapy*, 36: 477–82.

Aveline, M. (1988) in W. Dryden (ed.) *Group Therapy in Britain*, pp. 317–36. Buckingham: Open University Press.

Aveline, M. (1990) The group therapies in perspective, *Free Associations*, 19: 77–101.

Aveline, M. (1992) Leadership in brief training groups for mental health professionalism, in M. Aveline (ed.) *From Medicine to Psychotherapy*, pp. 140–54. London: Whurr.

Aveline, M. and Clarkson, P. (1997) The Psychotherapy and Counselling Oath, *Counselling*, 8: 11–12.

BACP (2002) *Ethical Framework for Good Practice in Counselling and Psychotherapy*. Rugby: British Association for Counselling and Psychotherapy.

Bion, W.R. (1961) *Experiences in Groups*. London: Tavistock.

Foulkes, S.H. and Anthony, E. (1957) *Group Psychotherapy: The Psychoanalytic Approach*. Harmondsworth: Penguin.

Rapaport, R.N. (1960) *Community as Doctor*. London: Tavistock.

Ratigan, B. and Aveline, M. (1988) Interpersonal group therapy, in M. Aveline and W. Dryden (eds) *Group Therapy in Britain*, pp. 45–64. Buckingham: Open University Press.

Whitaker, D.S. (1985) *Using Groups to Help People*. London: Routledge & Kegan Paul.

Yalom, I.D. (1995) Interpersonal learning, in *The Theory and Practice of Group Psychotherapy*, 4th edn, pp. 17–46. New York: Basic Books.

Yalom, I.D. and Lieberman, M.A. (1971) A study of encounter group casualties, *Archives of General Psychiatry*, 25: 16–30.

Yalom, I.D., Brown, S. and Bloch, S. (1975) The written summary as a group psychotherapy technique, *Archives of General Psychiatry*, 32: 605–13.

9 Ethics and supervision

Carol Shillito-Clarke

In the domains of counselling and the psychological therapies, 'supervision' or 'consultative support' describes an activity where one or more therapists discuss issues about their work, in order to reflect on that work and to have the work reflected on by one or more other professionals. Regular supervision of all therapeutic work is a requirement for all therapists while in training and for those members of the BACP and BPS Divisions of Clinical and Counselling Psychology while in practice. Other professional bodies require practitioners registered with them to use supervision when they feel in need of external support. While the need for supervision during training is agreed, the belief that supervision should be required after qualification is not universally supported (Lawton and Feltham 2000). Among those who do regard it as necessary, there is no consensus about what supervision is, how it should be conducted and who should do it.

In this chapter, reflecting my integrative approach, supervision is conceptualized as a formal, professional relationship that enables the participants to take a more objective view of all aspects of the therapist's work. It is an interpersonal learning space in which the therapist can stand back, reflect, reconsider and re-evaluate what is happening with the client, the relationship and with the therapy. It is also a 'play space' (Nahum 1993) in which the unthinkable may be thought and the unsayable may be said. I believe that it is important to recognize that the requirement for supervision after qualification does not imply that any therapist who experiences difficulties is incompetent or likely to behave unethically. Rather, it acknowledges the complexity of engagement in human interaction and the importance of support in the face of psychological burnout. It also acknowledges that therapeutic work is an ongoing learning process for the supervisor and the therapist as well as the client; everyone involved shares responsibility for the duty of care to the client.

Characteristics of supervision

The ethics of supervision are often considered to be the same as those for counselling and other psychological therapies, irrespective of the theoretical orientation. The primary purpose of supervision is a 'duty of care': to ensure that the therapeutic work is in the client's best interests. Those practitioners who supervise trainees or are employed as supervisors may be deemed to have some legal accountability for the therapist's work, though the extent of the 'vicarious liability' for the client of any supervisor has not yet been determined in English law (Bond 2000; Jenkins 2001). In addition to the ethical responsibility to the client, supervisors may be deemed to have a responsibility towards the therapist: to support and enhance their practice and to clarify the lines of responsibility for the work with the client. Awareness of the social context of the therapeutic work beyond the supervisor/therapist/client triangle may also be considered as an integral part of the principles of justice and social responsibility (BACP 2002).

In recognizing that supervision is a different activity from therapy, requiring different attitudes, knowledge and skills, the supervisor has an ethical responsibility to develop and maintain their own competence. This may include the use of consultancy for their supervisory work (BPS, DCoP 2001; BACP 2002). Because the supervisory process may reflect some of the interpersonal vulnerabilities of the therapeutic process, some authorities consider clinical supervision to be different from supervision offered by someone in a managerial position. Access to independent consultation is considered ethically appropriate for those in peer supervision or those supervised by their manager (BPS, DCoP 2001; BACP 2002).

There are many models of supervision (Inskipp and Proctor 1993, 1995; Holloway 1995; Carroll 1996a; Gilbert and Evans 2000; Hawkins and Shohet 2000; Page and Woskett 2002). How supervision is conducted depends on the professional backgrounds and theoretical orientations of the practitioners, the developmental needs of the therapist, the perceived needs of the client, the contract for therapeutic work, and the context and culture in which it takes place.

Supervision of work where the theoretical orientation reflects traditional scientific values is more likely to be task-oriented focusing on skills, goals, outcomes and quality assurance. Where the theoretical orientation reflects the humanistic values of cooperation and individual autonomy, supervision is more likely to concentrate on the processes between therapist and client, and supervisor and therapist (see Strawbridge, this volume). Where the practitioners are trained in different disciplines, have different understandings of contextual needs or have different theoretical orientations, careful negotiation of the purposes and desired outcomes of the supervision will be essential. For some therapists in training or in employment, there may be little choice of either the supervisor or supervision practice. This can increase the potential for ethical difficulties.

The practice of supervision may take many forms:

- Self-supervision – an internal process usually conducted by the therapist during and immediately after seeing a client.
- Individual supervision – one therapist working with a supervisor.
- Group and peer group supervision – a number of counsellors working together with or without a designated supervisor to consider each other's work.
- Live supervision – where one or more supervisors work with the therapist as they work with the clients, as in family therapy.

Many therapists may practise self-supervision. Some may choose to have more than one type of external supervision. Meetings with a supervisor may be held regularly or at the request of the therapist and the convenience of the supervisor. The formalization of all supervision arrangements and responsibilities in a contract is considered to be best practice (BACP 2002).

Formerly, training in and experience of working as a therapist under supervision were considered adequate qualifications to become a supervisor. In the past decade, it has become widely acknowledged that supervision is a process that requires specific knowledge and skills in addition to those required of a competent therapist. Training courses in supervision are now proliferating and research into supervision is also increasing (BACP holds a database of published work). As yet, there are no generally agreed standards for the practice of supervision against which competence can be assessed. This may change if the registration of therapists is accepted and if supervisors are held to greater legal and ethical account for their therapists' work.

Critical situations and their ethical resolution

The primary functions of supervision are ethical ones: the 'overseeing' of therapeutic practice to ensure that the best interests of the client are being met and the support of the therapist. Supervision itself is also a practice that must be conducted ethically. Critical situations for supervisors arise out of:

- the ethical duty of care to the client;
- the potential for misuse or abuse of power;
- the supervisor's responsibility to manage difference between all the participants and stakeholders;
- the need to balance the duty of care among several clients;
- the management of the multiplicity of relationships that surround the supervisory relationship.

Each of these is discussed separately below, but it must be remembered that they are interconnected: each invariably contains elements of one or more of the others. Factors such as the developmental status and experience of the therapist, bio-social and cultural differences (including race and sex), and the context in which therapist and supervisor work, must be taken into account in every case.

The extent to which a supervisor can protect clients from poor practice

A major concern for supervisors is their responsibility, and sometimes accountability, for the quality of the supervisee's work. This is a particularly difficult problem as, with the exception of live supervision, supervisors do not have direct access to that work. Additionally, most therapists carry a caseload that precludes an examination of every case, at each supervision session. The supervisor is therefore in a position of holding responsibility and accountability with little direct means of control.

> Gil is concerned about John's understanding of, and attention to, case management issues such as contracting, managing boundaries and keeping notes. His audiotapes suggest that John is good at counselling, but Gil is concerned about the potential for negligence. John will not accept there is a problem. He thinks that Gil is being fussy and unjustly critical.

In this vignette there is a difference of opinion between the supervisor and therapist about what constitutes good practice, which may be exacerbated by differences in training, theoretical values and personality, and the requirements of the context.

In assessing the quality of a therapist's work, the supervisor is reliant on the fidelity of the supervisory relationship and the integrity, resilience, humility and awareness of the therapist in presenting casework. There is no evidence of the work and the therapeutic relationship (process notes, tapes and so on) that cannot be manipulated if the therapist chooses to do so. Equally, the therapist is reliant on the supervisor's willingness to treat them with empathy, sincerity, respect, competence and fairness, particularly if the therapist is dependent on the supervisor's formal evaluation of their work.

In attempting to resolve differences of opinion about what constitutes good practice, the supervisor must draw on the principles of justice and non-maleficence, and model ethical reasoning. The supervisor needs to be able to evidence their perceptions and the conclusions drawn from them, debating with the therapist without becoming either defensive or aggressive. The supervisor also needs to be clear about the therapist's perception and reasoning in order to support their ethical development. In order to clarify and support their own ethical reasoning, the supervisor would be advised to discuss the situation with their own consultant and consider opportunities for external mediation if necessary.

A good resolution may not always be possible:

> A supervisor expresses her informed concern about the integrity of a therapist and his relationship with a vulnerable client. The therapist then informs the supervisor that he has cancelled his membership of the professional body and is leaving her supervision although he intends to continue his private practice.

In this situation, the termination of the contract absolves the supervisor from professional responsibility. However, she is left with the knowledge of potential harm to a client and no way of preventing it or calling the therapist to account. It is for this reason that those who employ practitioners or use their services need to be educated about the importance of professional practice ethics and accountability (Tjeltveit 1999).

Managing the power inherent in the supervisory relationship

Supervision entails responsibilities (see Wheeler and King 2001) and therefore power that must be exercised ethically. Spinelli (1994) contends that abuse in therapy arises from the misuse of power in the therapeutic relationship, particularly when the experience of power is perceived as weighted in favour of the therapist. In supervision, there is a parallel weighting in favour of the supervisor because of the duty of care to the client: the ultimate responsibility to make a formal complaint against a therapist who abuses a client.

Proctor (2002) suggests that there are three aspects of power in the therapeutic relationship and by extension in the supervisory relationship. These are:

- role power (ascribed by society and the therapeutic context to the role of the practitioner);
- societal power (from structural positions such as age, sex, race);
- historical power (each person's experience of power in their own relationships).

She argues that power is 'something that is present in the relationship rather than being the possession of one person; as bi-directional and influenced also by outside relationships; as inescapable and as potentially both positive and negative' (Proctor 2002: 136).

The exercise of role power to help another – to empower – is a cornerstone of therapy and supervision. For instance, directing a therapist who is impaired by illness or stress to take time out of work, or encouraging one who is struggling to undertake further training, would represent the benevolent exercise of power. However, the exercise of role power in the best interests of both client and therapist is not always easy to balance. Power denied cannot be managed and may be harmful (Page 1999). Uncertainty or a challenge to one's competence can lead to the misuse of power in the attempt to gain a better sense of control. As Guggenbühl-Craig (1971: 10) points out: 'In general the power drive is given freest rein when it can appear under the cloak of objective and moral rectitude'. A distinction must always be made between responsibility to, which accounts for the autonomy of the other, and responsibility *for*, which may devalue it.

Societal power and historical power are particularly complex as they vary with the individual relationships and context. Furthermore, both role and societal power have a historical dimension, dependent on previous personal and professional experiences of authority and discrimination. Although practitioners with some theoretical orientations may not consider it important, Dhillon-Stevens (2001) argues that supervisors and therapists should recognize the structural (or societal) dimensions of power in order to avoid oppressive and unethical practice.

In upholding the principles of justice and fidelity, supervisors need to be aware of, and able to work with, all three levels of power in their own relationship with the therapist; in the relationship between the therapist and the client; in the relationships with other 'stakeholders'; and in any reflections and resonance between these relationships (the parallel process).

> Carl offers supervision at reduced fees to a few trainees on placement in the institution where he works. One third-year student feels increasingly uncomfortable with his attitude to the short-term work she is doing and the theoretical arguments and interpretations he makes. She regards him as arrogant, sexist and patronizing but believes that she cannot challenge him because he is highly regarded by the institution and she is reliant on him for a reference. Carl is concerned about the student's competence, humility and openness to others' perceptions and ideas.

In this vignette, the balance of role and societal power are clearly weighted to the supervisor, although other factors, such as age and culture, may be important mediators. Both parties are caught in a stalemate of defending their own practice. Both may be reacting to perceived challenges to their own historical power. The help of an independent negotiator may be necessary.

Both supervisor and therapist have an ethical duty to be as aware as possible of their own potentially confounding processes. In some situations, for example when supervisor and therapist are friends, work colleagues or members of a supervision group, necessary censure of a therapist can be a difficult responsibility to fulfil. It is even harder for a therapist to challenge a supervisor. To place professional obligations over personal connections requires courage and integrity. If ethical supervision is to be achieved then a relationship of trust and honesty, paralleling that of the therapist and client, which recognizes the *shared* responsibility for success of the therapeutic practice, is critical. The therapist has a responsibility to exercise integrity, courage and honesty in disclosing potentially impaired, poor or incompetent practice. The supervisor has a responsibility to respect the therapist and not to humiliate or destructively criticize mistakes but to use their power to support and empower the therapist to reflect, learn and develop. Both have to question ignorance, prejudice and oppressive beliefs and attitudes in the other. Where the concern to avoid non-maleficent practice may override respect for individual autonomy, both at individual and institutional levels, care must be taken to avoid creating a 'culture of surveillance' (see Lawton and Feltham 2000).

Managing differences

Different people hold different values and expectations. Respect for others' differences is fundamental to good ethical practice but runs counter to the natural, and often very subtle, distrust of difference and difficulty in tolerating uncertainty. Wherever there are differences, there is the possibility that values will be assigned accordingly. The use (or abuse) of power in promoting the more valued difference is the likely consequence.

Differences abound in every relationship (sex, race, age, class, political affiliation, culture, sexual orientation, disability and so on). Personal life cannot be separated from the professional. The work of supervisors, in common with that of all professionals, is not only rooted in personal values but also shaped by the values of their professional training, theoretical approach and the requirements of the working context. No therapy is value free. All theoretical models include ideas about what constitutes psychological well-being. Different therapeutic systems will value the work (or 'treatment') done with the client differently. For instance, a supervisor may be more concerned with the demonstrable 'expertise' of the therapist, whereas the therapist is more concerned with the therapeutic relationship and process.

Supervisors have not only to be aware of, and work with the obvious differences between themselves and their supervisees, but also to work with the differences between each therapist and each of their clients and any contextual differences. Being alert to issues of difference and working with them ethically is therefore a major skill in supervision. The need for skill and awareness is multiplied when there are a number of participants involved, as in group or live supervision. It is the supervisor's ethical responsibility to the therapist, to address any differences in theory and practice and to negotiate an appropriate way of working. It may be particularly difficult for a therapist to question the supervisor, especially where the role and societal power differentials are significant.

At an organizational level, different professions, and even different domains within one profession, may operate different codes of ethics and have different ethical priorities. Such tensions will inevitably be replayed in supervision, and the supervisor may find themself having to defend a particular system rather than debating the issues and facilitating the therapist to reach their own ethical conclusions.

> Alex supervises three counsellors who work for an organization that is struggling financially. The counsellors have come under increasing pressure to reduce the number of sessions offered to each client. Alex, whose own training and theoretical orientation is different from the counsellors', can conceptualize ways in which some change could be made. Two of the three counsellors, however, argue that this would mean compromising their core model. They also argue that the clients surveyed are satisfied with the service they have had.

Many tensions arise in supervision because the different values and beliefs underlying the supervisory relationship are not made explicit. Mearns (1991) suggests that the majority of expectations and norms remain hidden from consciousness and therefore may not be voiced, to the detriment of the relationship. The key ethical questions for supervisors to ask of themselves and their supervisees might include the following:

- What assumptions am I making about this person's/organization's values?
- Whose values and criteria are directing this therapy?
- What differences might I/we be seeking to dismiss or ignore?
- How do I balance my autonomy with that of this other person?
- How do I work with a difference that challenges my self-esteem or competence?

As most therapists and supervisors invest a great deal of themselves in their work, any negative evaluation may challenge their self-esteem and sense of personal competence, as suggested in the earlier vignettes. Acknowledging difficulty in accepting differences may be particularly problematic and a source of ethical difficulty because it may be interpreted as a failure to act with equality, respect and the expectation of political correctness. However, as Ryde (2000: 47) argues: 'open supervision does not put into question the basic worth of the supervisee who reveals prejudiced or culturally insensitive attitudes. They could indeed be praised for their courage in being prepared to own up to difficult thoughts, feelings and beliefs. Having been voiced and explored, a genuine change of attitude is the most likely outcome.' For this to be a truly ethical learning experience, supervisors need to be prepared to admit their own prejudices openly as well.

Some supervisors may work only with therapists who share their own training and theoretical orientation. While this consistency of values and beliefs may be appropriate for trainees, it can lead to compliance and complacency in more experienced practitioners. There is a tendency to forget that different things help different people and that something that is beneficial to one may be detrimental to another. The therapist is not encouraged or challenged to question their practice and understanding from different perspectives. As a result, the process can become stagnant and devalued, and poor or unethical practice may be overlooked. It is perhaps even more important for practitioners who have few differences to ask themselves regularly: how else might this situation be construed theoretically, personally, professionally or contextually?

Balancing the duty of care to several 'clients'.

> Chris has a contract to supervise a team of counsellors employed by a psychology service. The counsellors' remit, which is funded by the primary care trust, is to provide six-session therapy in GP surgeries. In the supervision group, Pat discusses a serious concern about a young Asian woman. Sunita has been referred by her GP who is also a family friend, for help with anxiety and depression. She tells Pat she is newly married and fears she might be pregnant. Pat is anxious that Sunita may be at risk. Her husband and mother-in-law accompany her to the surgery but she does not want them to know what she is talking about. Chris is aware that the supervision group are divided in their evaluation of the situation and their values.

So far in this chapter, I have followed the custom of discussing supervision as if it were simply a triangular relationship in which *a* supervisor has responsibility for *a* therapist's work with *a* client (or clients if it is a couple or a family). In practice, this model is oversimplistic because it ignores many others who may have a legitimate interest in the efficacy of the therapy. It also overlooks the overt and covert levels of interaction and attempted influence between them. The BACP *Ethical Framework* defines a client as 'the recipient of any of [these] services' (BACP 2002: 5). Thus the client who comes for therapy (the primary client) is, by extension, a client of the supervisor, as is the therapist. Any person or organization that pays for the therapy and/or employs the practitioners in their respective capacities may also be deemed to be a client of their services. Such secondary clients, particularly when care of the primary client is shared, may have an interest or investment in the outcome of the therapy that is based on finance (employers or insurers), on medical responsibility (a referring GP or psychiatrist) or legal responsibility (for example the guardians of minors or those temporarily impaired).

All these clients have different relationships with the primary client and may have different views and expectations about the value of that therapy, the appropriate role of the therapist, and the preferred outcome. Many of their values and expectations, which may be dissonant, can impact on the way the client views therapy, the work of the therapist and the way that work is brought to supervision. This problem is compounded if the therapist is working with a couple or with a therapy group. Where care of the client is shared, or subject to scrutiny by others, the supervisor may become involved in boundary issues such as the disclosure of confidential information in supervision notes and other forms of interpersonal communications. Such boundary problems need to be considered and addressed by the supervisor from the outset (Walker and Clark 1999; BACP 2002).

In addition to the professional determinants of the limits of responsibility, it is also arguable that both supervisor and therapist have a broader, social ethical responsibility to be aware of others who may be affected by the probity of the therapist's work, for example partners, families, friends, social communities and professional bodies (Tjeltveit 1999; Hawkins and Shohet 2000; BPS, DCoP 2001; BACP 2002). In the depths of the involvement with the client or clients, it can be difficult for a therapist to hold a wider perspective on their work and to recognize other influences operating on the client or themself. As many writers suggest, it is one of the supervisor's responsibilities to hold these 'others' in awareness in the primary client's best interests. This may be done by, for example, reviewing potentially conflicting interests and values, and by encouraging the therapist's awareness of, and resistance to, not only overt and covert pressures to meet others' interests but also any personal bias and pressure the therapist may put on themself (Holloway 1995; Carroll 1996b; Hughes and Pengelly 1997; Gilbert and Evans 2000; Hawkins and Shohet 2000).

Managing the multiplicity of relationships in the supervision space

Just as the model of the supervisory triangle is an oversimplistic description of the influential relationships, so too is the conception of supervision as being contained within a specific time and space. Although supervisors are ethically prohibited from having sexual relationships with their supervisees and are advised against offering them therapy, they are not prohibited from having other professional or social relationships with them.

The world of therapy is relatively small and a supervisor's path may easily overlap with those of the therapists with whom they work, other professionals who know a therapist or client, or other stakeholders in the work under supervision. In a group setting, the chance that one person will recognize a client or someone connected to a client and therefore, by implication, the client, are increased.

Whenever boundaries overlap, they weaken and may become porous. This can create problems, particularly if the context of the meeting is different from that of the work. The situation is even more complicated when the client is also a therapist. When supervision boundaries are unclear or unreliable, there is a potential for mistakes and unethical practice that may be reflected or re-enacted in the work with the client. All interconnections have ethical implications for every practitioner and their clients' right to confidentiality.

Informed consent and choice are core values in promoting autonomy and respect for the work of therapy. The key to managing responsibilities in multiple relationships is through clear contracting between the significant parties from the start, recognizing that contracts may need to be reviewed and renegotiated as time passes or as the situation alters. The supervisor, by virtue of their role power, is usually recognized as having the greater share in initiating and directing the negotiations with each 'client' (BACP 2002). While a written agreement cannot cover every ethical eventuality, it demonstrates respect for each party's perspective and concerns, makes assumptions clear and clarifies where expectations of roles and responsibilities differ.

It is not always possible to predict at the start how a supervisory relationship may change over time and with circumstances. In the interests of non-maleficence, fidelity and justice, the needs of the professional relationship must always remain paramount. These principles may be hard to uphold when supervisor and therapist have powerful personal needs of the relationship that conflict with this duty of care to the client.

Emergent themes

Several themes arise from our exploration of the ethical issues of accountability, power difference and multiple relationships in supervision. They are:

- the ethical implications for supervision as therapeutic quality control;
- the need to recognize and be able to work with different values systems;
- the need for more training in supervision;

- a re-visioning of supervision as a forum for learning and continual development of ethical practice.

Supervision may be seen as the exercise of therapeutic ethics. Its primary function is an ethical one: the practice of therapy in the client's best interests. The process by which this is carried out must also be an ethical one. What constitutes the ethical duty of care to the client is a matter of interpretation. How this is defined and by whom will vary between and within different disciplines and theoretical approaches to therapy. In Chapter 1, Sheelagh Strawbridge emphasized the ethical tension between the approaches to therapy that emphasize 'doing-to' as opposed to 'being-with' the client.

The more objective, 'doing-to' approaches to therapy that have technical competence, problem resolution and evidence of effectiveness at their core, require supervision that focuses on goals, action plans and techniques, and is accountable for quality control. The supervisor will be expected to have greater expertise than the therapist and to take significant responsibility *for* the effectiveness of the therapy and the safety of the client. This can lead to an overvaluation of skills and qualifications at the expense of professional autonomy and the fidelity of the relationship. At worst, it can endorse a power imbalance through which the supervisor may abuse the supervisee. When there is an emphasis on supervision as scrutinizing practice to avoid mistakes there is a potential for a culture of shame and the consequent denial of problems to the supervisor to avoid censure. While a focus on non-maleficence may appear to secure ethical practice, there is little evidence for its support (Feltham 2000).

Conversely, supervision of a 'being-with' approach to therapy focuses on the work as expressed through the changing nature of the therapeutic relationship and on the way the therapist brings that into the supervision session. Practitioners who value the unique, subjective experience of 'being with' the client as necessary and sufficient for change, may deny the client's need for informed help. They may also disregard their ethical responsibility to others. Self-supervision, while valuable, cannot cover all the therapist's 'blind and deaf' spots, or access the many aspects of the interaction that occur out of their awareness. Expectations and assumptions about issues of accountability and responsibility for the work of the therapist must be made clear from the start, together with the means by which they will be enacted.

Ethical practice can never be guaranteed. We need to recognize the complexity of the therapeutic relationship and the human limitations of the therapist, however well trained and experienced. The importance of the relationship as a major variable in the effectiveness of therapy has been convincingly demonstrated (Roth and Fonagy 1996). It is reasonable to believe that the supervisory relationship has similar significance for the effectiveness of supervision. Therefore the work of the supervisor must be to work *with* the therapist to increase the efficacy of the therapeutic practice and to create a climate in which best ethical practice is valued.

Valuing the importance of a constructively critical supervision, Adams (2002: 207) points out: 'There is nothing intrinsic to supervision that makes it persecutory. These attributes are brought into it by the person in the role of the supervisor and the person in the role of the supervisee.' The therapist needs to be able to exercise humility in opening up their work to the scrutiny of others, and to value the opportunity to reflect on and be supported in further learning. Such exposure of professional vulnerability necessarily requires that the supervisor has the skills, abilities and personal qualities to create a secure base from which the therapist can stand back and reflect on the work, play with new ideas and learn. However facilitative the supervisor may wish to be, they must be able to hold authority when necessary and work constructively with the power dynamics of the various relationships.

In considering the issues discussed above, it becomes clear that a supervisor has considerable ethical responsibilities to the therapists with whom they work, their clients and the many other people who may be more or less implicated in the therapy. Holding and juggling such responsibilities requires that supervisors are trained and competent in the 'art and craft' of supervision and are committed to their own professional development. In addition to the relevant skills and theoretical knowledge, such competence also implies personal awareness and the ability and strength to model openness to making mistakes and learning from them. Good supervision is primarily an ongoing learning process and we have much to learn from our supervisees, however inexperienced, as well as senior consultants.

At this time, when there is no national agreement about appropriate training or the standards required of supervisors, there is no yardstick by which a supervisor can be evaluated as competent. This has repercussions for the recognition of the role of supervision within ethical therapy by both therapists and clients and the consequent employment of supervisors. It also calls into question the role and ethical responsibilities of the supervisor in cases of complaint and litigation against the therapist and, potentially, against the supervisor themself. The possible future registration of therapists will have further implications for supervisors and how they are valued.

If we are to promote supervision as an important part of ethical therapy, we need to demonstrate its value. Research into supervision, as a means of facilitating ethical practice, as well as the process and outcome of resolving ethical issues, is needed. As I have suggested elsewhere, there is also a need for more open acknowledgement of our own ethical mistakes and difficulties in therapeutic and supervision practice without the fear of being misjudged (Shillito-Clarke 2003). Ethical supervision, like ethical living, needs to become 'a process you go through so that as each new situation arises, the inclination to choose ethically is stronger in you, even if the right path is less clear' (Bell 2002: 36).

References

Adams, M. (2002) Reflections on reflection, *Journal of the Society for Existential Analysis*, 13(2).

BACP (2002) *Ethical Framework for Good Practice in Counselling and Psychotherapy*. Rugby: British Association for Counselling and Psychotherapy.

Bell, D. (2002) *Ethical Ambition: Living a Life of Meaning and Worth*. London: Bloomsbury.

Bond, T. (2000) *Standards and Ethics for Counselling in Action*, 2nd edn. London: Sage.

BPS, DoCP (2001) *Professional Practice Guidelines*. Leicester: British Psychological Society.

Carroll, M. (1996a) *Counsellor Supervision: Theory, Skills and Practice*. London: Sage.

Carroll, M. (1996b) *Workplace Counselling*. London: Sage.

Dhillon-Stevens, H. (2001) Anti-oppressive practice in the supervisory relationship, in M. Carroll and M. Tholstrup (eds) *Integrative Approaches to Supervision*. London: Jessica Kingsley.

Feltham, C. (2000) Counselling supervision: baselines, problems and possibilities, in B. Lawton and C. Feltham (eds) *Taking Supervision*

Forward: Enquiries and Trends in Counselling and Psychotherapy. London: Sage.

Gilbert, M. and Evans, K. (2000) *Psychotherapy Supervision in Context: An Integrative Approach*. Buckingham: Open University Press.

Guggenbühl-Craig, A. (1971) *Power in the Helping Professions*. Woodstock: Spring Publications, Inc.

Hawkins, P. and Shohet, R. (2000) *Supervision in the Helping Profession*, 2nd edn. Buckingham: Open University Press.

Holloway, E. (1995) *Clinical Supervision: A Systems Approach*. London: Sage.

Hughes, L., and Pengelly, P. (1997) *Staff Supervision in a Turbulent Environment: Managing Process and Task in Front-line Services*. London: Jessica Kingsley.

Inskipp, F. and Proctor, B. (1993) *The Art and Craft of Counselling Supervision. Part 1: Making the Most of Supervision*. Twickenham: Cascade.

Inskipp, F. and Proctor, B. (1995) *The Art and Craft of Counselling Supervision. Part 2: Becoming a Supervisor*. Twickenham: Cascade.

Jenkins, P. (2001) Supervisory responsibility and the law, in S. Wheeler and D. King (eds) *Supervising Counsellors: Issues of Responsibility*. London: Sage.

Lawton, B. and Feltham, C. (2000) *Taking Supervision Forward: Enquiries and Trends in Counselling and Psychotherapy*. London: Sage.

Mearns, D. (1991) On being a supervisor, in W. Dryden and B. Thorne (eds) *Training and Supervision for Counselling in Action*. London: Sage.

Nahum, T. (1993) Playing within the boundaries of supervision, *Australian Journal of Psychotherapy*, 12(1/2): 108–21.

Page, S. (1999) *The Shadow of the Counsellor: Working with the Darker Aspects of the Person, Role and Profession*. London: Routledge.

Page, S. and Woskett, V. (2002) *Supervising the Counsellor: A Cyclical Model*, 2nd edn. London: Sage.

Proctor, G. (2002) *The Dynamics of Power in Counselling and Psychotherapy: Ethics, Politics and Practice*. Ross-on-Wye: PCCS Books.

Roth, A. and Fonagy, P. (1996) *What Works for Whom: A Critical Review of Psychotherapy Research*. London: Guilford Press.

Ryde, J. (2000) Supervising across difference, *The International Journal of Psychotherapy*, 5(1): 37–48.

Shillito-Clarke, C.M. (2003) Ethical issues in counselling psychology, in R. Woolfe, W. Dryden and S. Strawbridge (eds) *Handbook of Counselling Psychology*, 2nd edn. London: Sage.

Spinelli, E. (1994) *Demystifying Therapy*. London: Constable.

Tjeltveit, A.C. (1999) *Ethics and Values in Psychotherapy*. London: Routledge.

Walker, R. and Clark, J.J. (1999) Heading off boundary problems: clinical supervision as role management, *Psychiatric Services*, 5(11): 1435–9.

Wheeler, S. and King, D. (eds) (2001) *Supervising Counsellors: Issues of Responsibility*. London: Sage.

10 Forms of ethical thinking and practice

Derek Hill and Caroline Jones

If there was a hypothesis to be tested in the process of compilation of this book it concerned the idea that practitioners' perceptions about the nature of the client–therapist relationship, and about the potential and the limitations of therapeutic interventions, are strongly influenced by the form of therapy being delivered, *and that those perceptions affect the ways in which ethical issues are considered*. Rather than asking contributors to argue the merits of the approach to ethical issues and matters of good practice adopted by fellow practitioners within their therapeutic modality, they were asked to describe the issues they faced and the ways in which they tackled them. That editorial decision was certainly influenced by an awareness that postmodern thinking is having its impact in psychotherapeutic circles (see Chapters 5 and 7). An introduction to postmodern ideas is offered by Appignanesi and Garratt (1999) and discussed in terms of therapies by Flaskas (2002) who describes postmodernism as 'an oppositional frame to modernism, and its parameters are the parameters of critique. . . . Not this [not modernism]' (p. 20).

While the ethicists agree that the very survival of 'civilization' depends on people interacting in a genuinely ethical manner, postmodernism calls for the replacement of (modernist) ethical thinking based on universal principles and truths by concerns about *practical philosophy*, that is concerns about human *praxis* (patterns of interactive behaviour) (Madison and Fairbairn 1999).

The foregoing chapters have thus focused on therapists of various kinds *in action* and upon the thinking that both underpins and is the product of that activity. This chapter explores the extent to which the editors' hypothesis has been validated and goes on to consider the implications of the learning that may be drawn from Chapters 1–9, the work of contributors who are all expert in their chosen area of specialization.

What are practitioners' concerns regarding ethics and good practice?

Chapters 2–9 describe in some detail the critical issues, and others that are emergent, in disparate therapeutic modalities and, in the case of Lina Kashyap's chapter, in a markedly different cultural context. Two observations can be made here. First, it is evident that several ethical issues arise in all of the forms of therapy described by the contributors. Second, postmodernism may well be exerting subtle influences as a result of the adoption of ideas such as multiple realities, co-construction of stories, and concerns about *the question of* (whose) *ethics*, but in terms of day-to-day practice, ethical thinking generally appears to remain firmly grounded in modernist ideas: principles and values.

If we step away from a detailed consideration of different therapeutic modalities, the BACP offers us an intriguing insight into the concerns of UK-based therapists. The Association's members have access to an advisory service about ethical issues and it has recently published information about its use (BACP 2003).

Over the period surveyed (April to December 2002), and in round figures, the number of inquiries received from practitioners working in different settings were: organizations 490, private 380, education 250, medical 140 and EAP 15. Even allowing for some membership categories being several times larger than others, EAP inquiries are strikingly few and one is left wondering whether there may be some connection between the degree to which client contracts are made explicit and are formalized and low demand for the advisory service.

Further statistics about the same BACP advisory service appear to support that conjecture – that large numbers of inquiries arise out of issues related to client–therapist contracts. Inquiries received were categorized as relating to boundaries, confidentiality, contracts, legal issues, records or supervision, and no other category of inquiry achieves even half of the numbers of those to do with contracts.

Contracting issues

Examined in the light of that observation, Chapters 2–9 reveal a shared emphasis given to discussion of the thinking that contributes to the establishment and maintenance of working relationships between therapists, clients and, in many instances, significant third parties which enable therapeutic purposes to be served. A rather closer examination of those accounts makes evident the great care and attention given to setting up those relationships, to the complexities of the processes of securing the *informed consent* of clients and other parties involved, and to ensuring that what has been negotiated and agreed is made explicit to all concerned. The chapters also make clear the fact that the agreements or contracts initially established are far from comprehensive and that, in many modalities, there is an expectation that they will be renegotiated again and again during the course of the therapy. Those contracts are, quite literally, starting points. But if they fail to take into account key influences internal or external to the therapy, or if they are not owned by all the parties involved, they can prove a source of difficulty, distress, or even the breakdown of the relationships they purport to underpin.

Chapter by chapter, the book's contributors set out what their experience has taught them are the (likely) influences that need attention when contracting. All are at pains to make clear that the contract must be jointly owned. Each explains, in a way congruent with their theoretical and philosophical stance, the strategies they use to try to secure the informed consent of clients and other parties. Those strategies differ significantly and, as is made particularly clear in Chapter 7, depend heavily upon choices made about what Sheila Strawbridge (Chapter 1) quotes as two modes of being-in-relation 'I–It' and 'I–Thou' (Buber 1958) and the related distributions of power between therapist and clients. Whether or not the therapist elects to interact as a technical expert or as a person-in-relationship, informed consent presents problems for both therapist and clients. No one involved can confidently predict the nature of the content, the processes, or the outcomes of therapy. The therapist has the insights offered by training, casework experience and the modality's codes of good practice; the clients have their stories and perceived needs, some part of which will have been shared with the therapist but, whatever the preferred language for explaining the nature of the situation, the fact is that no one is equipped to give irrevocable informed consent to a contract spanning more than a session or two. This fact has several implications.

First, such contracts need to embody the primary characteristics of the therapeutic relationship intended by, and within the competence of, the therapist and wanted by the clients, since they must be the fixed points around which everything else is built. This may seem to be an invitation to plunge into the complexities of the nature of therapeutic work, but as the chapters of this book demonstrate, the *primary* characteristics are few and simple, though not always easily articulated in ways that chime with the clients' beliefs and values. If effectively expressed, they will answer the client's question, 'How is my humanity going to be acknowledged and valued?'

Second, these contracts need to be an explicit response to the clients' needs and expectations. Those needs and expectations may be ill-formed and even ill-informed at an early stage of contact with a therapist. However, the issue is that they must be respectfully addressed.

Third, what is initially agreed must make explicit provision for review and renegotiation of the contract – not just an acknowledgement of the possibility of change but an agreement about the ways in which it can be achieved. The chapters of this book are full of descriptions of this dynamic aspect of therapy. Styles of working and the language used differ, but change in contracts is everywhere. It is seen that not all changes in contracts result from formal and explicit negotiation. The intimacy of the therapeutic relationship can result, as in other close relationships, in short-cuts being used and assumptions being made. The 'understandings' thus achieved have the potential to offer great benefits but, if not monitored and validated, can also be the downfall of a therapeutic relationship. There is also the risk of collusive avoidance, when issues that may impede or block therapeutic work are not addressed by those involved. In such circumstances, what Carol Shillito-Clarke has to say (Chapter 9) about the role and workings of supervision is relevant, as is the discussion of the processes fostered by systemic workers (Chapter 7) to do with 'self-reflexivity' and 'relational reflexivity' (Burnham 1993).

That the contracts being discussed signpost the therapeutic relationship will be evident. But they are also 'works in progress', evolving so as to keep the therapeutic relationship 'fit for task'. As such, they are themselves potent therapeutic agents, jointly constructed prescriptions for purposive, effective persons-in-relationship or, from another perspective, mutually transmutative relationships.

No doubt there are more thorough-going analyses of contracting and informed consent. This one, written in the context of 'forms of ethical thinking' has deliberately avoided the word 'ethics'. Why? Because it is the authors' conviction that what is being discussed is the practical politics of therapy. We believe that both therapist and client have their attention focused on finding good, workable solutions to the difficulties-in-living faced by the client. Nonetheless, the discussion has been about how to create an ethical framework for a working relationship that, over time, will be fleshed out and richer in meanings, becoming both complex and powerfully creative. That, to our minds, affirms therapy as a *fundamentally* ethical enterprise.

Discussion about setting up and working with contracts leads on to some thought-provoking comparisons. Samaritans (Chapter 3) may only have contact with their 'callers' once, yet they have an enviable reputation for the effectiveness (and by implication the ethical quality) of their service. Joan Guénault describes how, in the minutes or hours of a single phone call, the caller and the Samaritan establish and refine their working relationship – and much of that is achieved as a result of the volunteer's consistent valuing, caring, listening response to the caller, and the caller's growing intensity of engagement in their dialogue, rather than through extensive overt negotiation. Perhaps that process is more readily understood if it is remembered that Samaritans has a simply expressed yet potent public image – they are there to listen. Appendix 2 indicates the thinking and the ethical stance that sustains that image and that permits the organization's callers to have an intuitive grasp of the contract on offer – an intuition that is confirmed by the experience of talking to the volunteer.

Online therapists may also have limited 'contact' with their clients. However, as Kate Anthony and Stephen Goss make clear (Chapter 4), there could hardly be a starker contrast between the elaborate contracting the responsible online practitioner is obliged to engage in and the way in which a Samaritan responds to a caller. Those authors indicate at least several of the reasons for that difference: 'the emergence of email and Internet chat as means of conducting therapy in 1995 was client led' (p.50); 'the ability to communicate globally is one of the most important features of email and IRC' (p.53); 'even very basic terms such as what a potential client understands by the term "counsellor", "psychotherapist" or "psychologist" may differ immensely' (p.53). Those factors, together with the uncertain competences and trustworthiness (notwithstanding elaborate websites) of some of those who advertise services online, create quite different mind-sets in both clients and therapists *from the outset*. Whether, and in what way, those initial mind-sets exert a continuing influence on therapists' and clients' thinking about ethical issues and, thus, on the nature of the online therapy provided, merits close investigation. The question here is not about 'better than' and 'worse than' but has to do with gaining an understanding of the ways particular sets of contextual factors may shift the emphasis given to different values and ethical principles, and the balance between 'doing the right thing' and 'ends justifying means'.

A further cause for close attention to the detail of a contract is to be found in the accounts of contracting with couples (Chapter 5) and family groupings (Chapter 7), the latter account showing that different and distinct contracts may exist simultaneously with different family members to the benefit of all concerned.

Lina Kashyap presents a very different perspective on contracting (Chapter 6). In a vast country in which a number of different religions and cultures exert powerful influences, and traditional patterns of social organization permeate urban as well as rural communities, counselling is striving to redefine itself so as to provide an effective bridge between the aspirations and expectations of the modernizers, not least those influenced by India's feminist thinkers and campaigners, and the interest that the older generation, and many men, have in preserving power differentials and traditional roles. It is impossible to separate the struggle for change and 'better' solutions in the counselling room and that which goes on in the community at large.

Counselling itself in India is not without risk to the practitioner: 'addressing the issue of sex inequality publicly may also mean threatening the status quo in their personal lives.' (p.98) Meeting clients whose expectation is that they will receive advice, not to mention exhortations and coercion, and who anticipate '[an] emphasis . . . on maintaining the family bond at *all costs*' (editors' emphasis) (p.91), the counsellor may be faced with the dilemma that their personally and professionally espoused values are unacceptable to the clients and that, if any assistance is to be accepted, it must reflect both the values of the (client's) community, and its custom and practice in terms of the form of intervention provided. Those are no minor adjustments (for the counsellor), and may arise in the context of a client struggling with life and death issues and an overload of casework for the counsellor.

Lina Kashyap writes about the need to replace largely western intervention models with alternatives that address Indian realities. The dilemma referred to above makes it clear that the purposes and responsibilities of a 'counsellor' working in India may very well need to be significantly different from those that would be recognized in the UK – a redefinition of the boundary between counselling and social work? An examination of Appendix 3 will suggest the likely nature of the ethical framework within which such counsellors might be expected to work. What is apparent is that when negotiating a way of working with a client, those counsellors will be acutely aware of their role in society and the ways in which any envisaged intervention will impact on the community as well as on the client individually. Social reform and personal service seem inseparable. This prompts a question: have the purposes and priorities adopted by some forms of therapy largely disengaged them from the processes of social change?

John Burnham, Suzanne Cerfontyne and Joan Wynn write (Chapter 7) of a situation in which the therapeutic value of work with clients was being threatened by external constraints: the requirements of social services, the police and the referring agencies (p.107). The systemic therapists renegotiated the terms of the referral so as to be able to offer the clients the chance (and choice) to access the help that they might want. That casework vignette suggests that by being ready to involve third parties in contract negotiation it may be possible to perform a doubly beneficial function: effective therapy for the client and a significant educative input into the social matrix in which clients and therapists live.

Other issues?

Unlike the codes and frameworks of ethics and good practice formally adopted and published by the professional bodies, client–therapist contracts are generally far from comprehensive (Sills 1997: 216–20). Typically, the issues not mentioned explicitly are those which it is expected will have no impact of the therapy. Legal issues, practitioner's fitness (health, alcohol, drugs, competence), organizational issues and multiple relationships, among others, may not be addressed. The BACP statistics (2003) show that such issues may actually be confronted during the course of therapy and become major causes of concern. There is thus an argument for more comprehensive contracts, and many practitioners and service delivery organizations include in their contracts with clients a reference to the formal code or framework under which they work.

Contracts, and the thinking underlying them, have been shown to vary in nature from modality to modality because of the different sets of ambient issues being addressed. Issues that are atypical of a modality, and not featured in particular contracts, appear to elicit rather similar responses within the forms of therapy described in this book. Unfamiliarity with the ramifications of the issue may oblige the practitioner to seek (expert) advice. An awareness that there is no pre-existing position on the matter agreed by client and therapist can generate a need to offer the client information before seeking, wherever possible, to adopt a shared response to the matter. There remain those issues which it is either inappropriate or impossible to raise with the client.

Caroline Jones (Chapter 2) highlights the need for the counsellor employed by the same organization as her clients to take direct, and at times unilateral, responsibility for preventing dual relationships from generating troublesome conflicts of interest (p.22). Mark Aveline (Chapter 8) illustrates the therapist's unilateral action in expelling a member of a therapy group (p.132). Kate Anthony and Stephen Goss (Chapter 4) describe *therapists'* decisions not to work with potential online clients whose cultures are both very dissimilar and unfamiliar (p.54). It will be noted that these situations stem directly from the kind (modality, medium) of therapy being offered. The thinking that lies behind those decisions may be couched in the language of risk assessment – evaluations of the probability that particular courses of action will result in unmanageable conflicts of interest – situations in which none of the parties benefit. On the other hand, there will be occasions when, for want of information about, or understanding of, a situation, the practitioner falls back on 'good practice' and duty. Almost of necessity, thinking of the latter kind will have a defensive quality whereas the former can very often throw up creative outcomes – a contrast in uses of ethical thinking that we return to later in this chapter.

If alone in the ways just mentioned, forms of ethical thinking differ between and within therapeutic modalities. That being the case, it is appropriate to ask what we may learn from the practices within the different modalities that will enhance ethical thinking in our own practice.

Forms of ethical thinking and their impact on practice

The foregoing sections of this chapter reflect the facts revealed in other parts of this book: modality, medium and social context all dispose practitioners to view ethical issues through different lenses and to give different priorities to the values and principles that are held in common in the therapeutic world as being the starting points for ethical thinking. The evidence that this book presents is that which has been provided by highly regarded and expert practitioners. Readers will be aware that not all practice, and not all ethical thinking, is of the quality documented here. Why? First of all, because expertise gives our contributors a technical *dexterity* that enables them to find effective interventions that circumvent some ethical dilemmas. A good illustration of that dexterity is to be found in John Burnham's, Suzanne Cerfontyne's and Joan Wynn's account of the way that a constraint imposed on therapy with family members by one of those members was accommodated (p.114). Second, because this book's contributors have highly developed skills deriving from the notion that therapy is *fundamentally* an ethical enterprise. Ethical considerations are not a 'bolt-on' addition demanded by ideas about the professions, but lie at the heart of the work. Returning to the same casework vignette (p.114) – certainly there is evidence of dexterity but more than that, there is evidence of *creativity*. A constraint, and an ethical challenge, was perceived not so much as a threat to the therapeutic process but *as the opportunity for ethical thinking and the insights of a theoretical approach to work together to create a new dynamic within the case*. It is suggested that it was the alertness to ethical issues which prompted that creativity, realized through a technical dexterity. The family concerned discovered a new and rewarding richness in their relationships as a result – and that is the nature of *creativity*.

Examples of that creativity can be found in this book's other chapters. That evidence allows us to propose that the source of creativity in therapeutic practice is a constant and central consideration of ethical issues – by both therapist and client(s). Sheelagh

Strawbridge writes that 'ethical thinking [is] central to the process of therapy' (p.4). We want to propose that it is the *essence* of therapeutic work. What makes therapeutic processes quintessentially human and a force for good is its preoccupation with persons-in-relationships and the metric by which those relationships are valued.

How do practitioners acquire ethically inspired good practice?

The simple answer has to be by devoting themselves to the study of themselves and others in relationship and by making explicit those personal qualities, values and ethical principles which inspire those relationships with *creativity* – a synergistic quality that makes those involved more human than before. Sheelagh Strawbridge refers to the 'marginalization of ethical thinking' and calls for the integration of training in theory, practice and ethical thinking (p.3). Caroline Jones sees the new forms of formal declaration of professional bodies' ethical stance as important contributions to the task, and looks for new ethical challenges to be addressed by clients, therapist and society at large in concert (p.31). Joan Guénault regards the Samaritans' mission, vision and values statement (see Appendix 2) as an important touchstone for its volunteers, and sees its evaluated selection/induction procedure, and trainee group activities, as rich resources for its workers (p.36). Kate Anthony and Stephen Goss, discussing online therapy, spoke of no one having any rules or guidelines in the initial development period, but assert that 'considerable experience is required before the transfer to this new environment can be made' (p.55). Derek Hill (Chapter 5) identifies the need to develop a capacity for reflexivity, the support of carefully thought-through guidance, attention to contemporary thought about ethics (postmodernism), and an integration of ethical, theoretical and practice training as stepping stones to ethically based competence. Lina Kashyap (Chapter 6) describes a burgeoning world of counselling in India and lays great stress on acceptance of difference, a sensitivity to the values and mores of others, and the development of a capacity to see the counselling enterprise in the context of major change in society and the context of the assumptions made about power differentials in the multivarious society. The systemic therapists John Burnham, Suzanne Cerfontyne and Joan Wynn (Chapter 7), have a fully elaborated approach to ethical issues and advocate trainees' attention to contemporary thinking about ethics and postmodern philosophy and commend characteristic features of their practice as the means to develop ethically based competence – 'didactic teaching about ethical principles, processes and postures as well as codes of ethics. Integration in practice through live supervision, reflections during videotape review and rehearsals through role play' (p.105). In group therapy, Mark Aveline sees a plethora of regulatory bodies influencing his work but comments on their 'weak constraint compared with the therapist's internalized ethic, the personal, private undertaking that is made in every therapy' (p.123), and quotes his own personal ethical code while noting that in daily practice his co-therapist is an important source of an other-input into, and other-view on groups' processes. Not surprisingly, Carol Shillito-Clarke, writing about supervision, acknowledges a 'duty of care: to ensure that the therapeutic work is in the client's best interests' (p.139) and sees among the many models of supervision a common theme to do with the supervisor's primary responsibilities being ethical ones (p.141). Also, aware of an unresolved legal question about 'vicarious liability', she recognizes problems associated with the supervisor's ultimate sanction – withdrawal of supervision. Supervision takes place in the context of what is often a network of professional and managerial relationships. Modelling management of those relationships for the supervisee is one of the supervisor's tasks. (Ethical) tasks with experienced therapists and trainees are recognized as being different. Supervisors must take a continuing responsibility for their own ongoing professional development. And she concludes that, 'ethical supervision, like ethical living, needs to become "a process you go through so that as each new situation arises, the inclination to choose ethically is stronger in you, even if the right path is less clear" (Bell 2002: 36).'

Developing the capacities of therapists to undertake ethically inspired good practice thus seems a daunting task. The processes of selection, induction, training, trainee practicum, supervision, peer consultation and ongoing professional development must all be involved. Personal moral qualities, the values of therapy, and its ethical principles all demand attention (BACP 2002). However, a profoundly human motivation makes that task feasible: the desire of practitioners and others to be experienced by their fellows as a *creative* influence (and here is not the place to debate what creative means in a community wrestling with postmodern conceptualizations).

How might psychological therapies be made more reliably ethical in nature?

In one sense, the answer to that question has already been offered in the last subsection of this chapter. From another perspective, the question is about the implications of a contemporary debate about the professionalization of those who offer psychological therapies. Some say that full professional status and the associated regulation is the answer. Others, in favour of the non-expert therapist, see professionalization, as currently understood, as the downfall of therapy (House 2003). Our perspective is a *both–and* view. The evidence drawn from good practice offered by this book makes clear the place for formal codes and frameworks of ethics and good practice, and for practitioners to be challenged to account for their actions in terms of those criteria. Our own thinking, and that of authors who challenge the idea of professionalization and all that it currently implies, is based, with Mark Aveline (p.123), on the notion that reliably ethical services derive from *personal* ethical stances; from insights into self, others and the nature of relationships; and from an experience of, and a commitment to, finding ways to (help others to) live creatively.

Whatever the modality, medium or social context of our therapeutic enterprise we see practitioners challenged to achieve that purpose by what we regard as one of humankind's most powerful motivations: to be experienced by others as people who seek to live and relate creatively, and to offer those we touch the chance of synergistic expansion of our shared humanity.

References

Appignanesi, R. and Garratt, C. (1999) *Introducing Postmodernism*. Cambridge: Icon Books.

BACP (2002) *Ethical Framework for Good Practice in Counselling and Psychotherapy*. Rugby: British Association for Counselling and Psychotherapy.

BACP (2003) *EPN Newsletter 2002/3*. Rugby: British Association for Counselling and Psychotherapy.

Bell, D. (2002) *Ethical Ambition: Living a Life of Meaning and Worth*. London: Bloomsbury.

Buber, M, (1958) *I and Thou*, trans. R.G. Smith. Edinburgh: T. & T. Clark.

Burnham, J (1993) Voices from the training Context, a special edition of *Human Systems: The Journal of Systemic Consultation and Management*, 4.

Flaskas, C. (2002) *Family Therapy beyond Postmodernism*. Hove: Brunner–Routledge.

House, R. (2003) *Therapy beyond Modernity: Deconstructing and Transcending Profession-centred Therapy*. London: Karnac.

Madison, G. and Fairbairn, M. (eds) (1999) *The Ethics of Postmodernity: Current Trends in Continental Thought*. Evanston, IL: Northwestern University Press.

Sills, C. (ed.) (1997) *Contracts in Counselling*. London: Sage.

APPENDIX 1
Useful addresses

Association for Family Therapy
12A Executive Suite
St James Court
Wilderspool Causeway
Warrington
WA4 6PS
Telephone: 01925 444414
Email: s.kennedy@aft.org.uk
www.aft.org.uk

British Association for Counselling and Psychotherapy
BACP HOUSE 35–37 Albert Street
Rugby
CV21 2SG
Telephone: 0870 443 5252
Fax: 0870 443 5160
Minicom: 0870 443 5162
Email: bacp@bacp.co.uk
www.bacp.co.uk

British Association of Psychotherapists
37 Mapesbury Road
London
NW2 4HJ
Telephone: 020 8452 9823
Fax: 020 8452 5182
Email: mail@bap-psychotherapy.org
www.bap-psychotherapy.org

British Association for Sexual and Relationship Therapy
PO Box 13686
London
SW20 9ZH
Telephone/fax: 0208 543 2707
Email: info@basrt.org.uk.
www.basrt.org.uk

The British Psychological Society
St Andrews House
48 Princess Road East
Leicester
LE1 7DR
Telephone: 0116 254 9568
Fax: 0116 254 0787
Email: mail@bps.org.uk
www.bps.org.uk

Confederation of Scottish Counselling Agencies
18 Viewfield Street
Stirling
FK8 1UA
Telephone: 01786 475140
Fax: 01786 446207
Email: cosca@compuserve.com
www.cosca.org.uk

Department of Health Publications
PO Box 777
London
SE1 6XH
Fax: 01623 724524
Email: doh@prolog.uk.com

Prevention of Professional Abuse Network
1 Wyvil Court
Wyvil Road
London
SW8 2TG

Telephone: 020 7622 6334
Fax: 020 7622 9788
Email: info@popan.org.uk
www.popan.org.uk

Relate
Herbert Gray College
Little Church Street
Rugby
CV21 3AP
Telephone: 01788 573241
Fax: 01788 535007
Email: enquiries@relate.org.uk
www.relate.org.uk

Samaritans
The Upper Mill
Kingston Road
Ewell
KT17 2AF
Telephone (Textphone): 020 8394 8300
Fax: 020 8394 8301
Email: admin@samaritans.org
www.samaritans.org

Tata Institute of Social Sciences
PO Box 8313
Sion Trombay Road
Deonar
Mumbai 400 088
India
www.tiss.edu

Telephone Helplines Association
4 Deans Court
St Paul's Churchyard
London
EC4V 5AA

United Kingdom Association of Humanistic Psychology Practitioners
Box BCM AHPP
London
WC1N 3XX
Telephone: 08457 660326
Fax: 01348 840845
www.ahpp.org

UK Council for Psychotherapy
167–169 Great Portland Street
London
W1W 5PF
Telephone: 020 7436 3002
Fax: 020 7436 3013
Email: ukcp@psychotherapy.org.uk
www.psychotherapy.org.uk

APPENDIX 2
Samaritans: Mission, Vision and Values

The Mission

The Samaritans is available 24 hours a day to provide confidential emotional support for people who are experiencing feelings of distress or despair, including those which may lead to suicide.

The Vision

The Samaritans' vision is for a society in which:

- fewer people die by suicide
- people are able to explore their feelings
- people are able to acknowledge and respect the feelings of others.

The Values

The Samaritans' values are based on these beliefs:

- the importance of having the opportunity to explore difficult feelings
- that being listened to, in confidence, and accepted without prejudice, can alleviate despair and suicidal feelings
- that everyone has the right to make fundamental decisions about their own life, including the decision to die by suicide.

APPENDIX 3
Declaration of Ethics for Professional Social Workers

Preamble

The Declaration of Ethics for Professional Social Workers is intended to serve as a guide to the members of the social work profession. Social work profession involves application of secular and value-based, scientific and systematic knowledge and skills of working with people, obtained through formal education, in the service of others, by way of practice, administration, education and research. Professional social workers are those who have obtained minimally a bachelor's/master's degree in social work and, thus, base their work on professional knowledge, values and skills. A document on ethics for professional social workers is needed in order to ensure self regulation rather than government control, guide professionals in resolving ethical dilemmas, protect the public from incompetent professionals and protect professionals from litigations.

The basic values of social work profession are human dignity and self worth of every person, people's participation and self determination, equality, freedom and justice. Values of the Indian social work profession have evolved as a combination of influence of the requirements of professional social work and the Indian social values. In the Indian society, families and communities are important contexts for relationships and the Indian culture are holistic and wisdom-oriented and emphasise duties. The social work values in India are influenced by humanism of the Bhakti movement, Swarajya and Lokniti of the Sarvodaya movement and values of socialism, secularism and democracy promoted by the Constitution of India.

The results of the recent trends towards liberalisation, privatisation and globalisation, have led to environmental devastation, social displacement and the weakening of cultural and biological diversity. These trends have resulted in increased unemployment, indebtedness and abject poverty. Globalisation has also led to the diminishing role of the state and increased emphasis on role of the voluntary organisations in the field of welfare. The emerging civil society approaches to counter globalisation are action groups, resulting in the new social movements, aiming towards sustainable and people-centred development. These approaches value the ideologies of equity or recognition of differences, diversity and pluralism; democratic pluralism; local self governance, and peaceful collaborative social dynamics. Social work profession has a very significant role to play in solidarity with people-centred ideologies and groups, at the national and the international levels. The profession recognises that marginalised people need to be empowered so that they have control over self as well as the resources which determine power. This process aims at systemic change as an imperative for redistributive justice.

Based on the values of professional social work, Indian social values and the emerging values of the civil society approaches, this Declaration provides a value framework and pledge and best ethical practices to guide the conduct of professional social workers with reference to responsibilities to self and the profession, people in need, society and the state, co-workers and employing organisations and social work education and research. In its practical application, the entire Declaration must be viewed holistically, and contextualised. Ethical issues/problems may also be analysed on the basis of the intent, the nature, and the consequences of the action.

The Declaration needs to be widely disseminated, discussed, translated into practice and made part of the professional culture. The value framework may be used to take a pledge at the graduating ceremonies in institutions of social work education. The Declaration needs to be reviewed and renewed, at least once in five years. The Declaration may be converted into a Code of Ethics when a council for professional social work is set up to monitor it.

Value framework and pledge

As a professional social worker, I pledge to inculcate and promote the following values in myself, in the profession, in the organisations I work with and in the society.

1. I pledge to perceive and accept people as having inherent worth and dignity, irrespective of their attributes and achievements, having the capability of change and development; and
   I pledge to perceive people as part of the scheme of nature, needing to live in harmony with other forms of life.
2. I pledge to work towards the well-being of all people, through the achievement of the following goals:
   - Basic human needs such as food and water security, health, livelihood, shelter, education, environmental security, family and community identity and interdependence, to be met as human rights;
   - Democratic pluralism in the socio-economic systems such as family, community, state, market and media;
   - Equity and equality, non-hierarchy, non-discrimination and democratic pluralism of human groups in terms of attributes such as race, nationality, colour, caste, religion, tribe, language, regional origin, gender, sexual orientation and other such factors, and condemnation of marginalisation and segregation among them; and
   - Social, economic, political and legal justice, ensuring universal and equitable access to essential resources and protective safeguards for the marginalised people.
3. I pledge to work with people, guided by the following values:
   - Honesty, personal integrity and accountability;
   - Solidarity and partnership with the marginalised people;
   - People's participation and self determination;
   - Cooperation and collaboration, instead of competition and confrontation, as the principles of interaction; and
   - Peace and non-violence for resolving conflicts with self, others and the environment.

Best ethical practices

Responsibilities to Self and the Profession

Professional social workers:

- Constantly seek an awareness of themselves and change their attitudes and behaviour, which negatively affect their work.
- Are sensitive to and respect the feelings and thinking of others, understand behaviours, avoid stereotypes and recognise uniqueness in every person.
- Accept with humility and openness, the need to learn and imbibe the spirit of inquiry to constantly update their knowledge base and intervention strategies.
- Base their practice upon relevant knowledge and in consonance with the changing socioeconomic, geographical and cultural context.
- Use their knowledge, authority and status as professionals, for the well-being of people and not misuse these for personal gains.
- Intervene into the personal affairs of another individual only with his/her consent, except when they must act to prevent injury to him/her or to others, in accordance with the legal provisions.
- Constantly review the social work profession and work towards its development, in order to ensure its credibility, integrity and relevance.
- Work to promote networking among social work professionals, other professionals and like-minded individuals and organisations, at the micro- and macro-levels, for people-centred development.
- Work towards promoting and strengthening of professional associations, which are committed to the improvement of the standards of professional practice, through active membership and participation.

Responsibilities to people in need

Professional social workers:

- Are committed and accountable to the marginalised and disadvantaged people.
- Empathise with people they work with, and thereby respect and give credence to their life experiences.
- Do not label them because of the problematic situation that they may be facing, but see their strengths and enable them to work on them.
- Nurture a relationship with people to promote mutual understanding of diverse cultures and life experiences.
- Work towards the promotion of social justice by consistently denouncing all kinds of oppression and discrimination.
- Work towards changing the systemic forces, which marginalise people, on behalf of and in partnership with them.
- Respect people's right for self determination, and ensure their participation in decision making about their life situation.
- Facilitate people's access to opportunities and resources and empower them to work towards their goals by encouraging the formation of people's organisations.
- Share with people, accurate and relevant information regarding the extent and nature of help available to them, which includes opportunities, rights, strengths, limitations and risks associated with the intervention.
- Inform people and obtain their consent before observing, recording or reporting their life situation, except in impossible circumstances.
- Keep confidential, all matters shared by them, and inform them about the limits of privileged communication in a given situation.
- Facilitate people's access to official records concerning them, and while doing so, take due care to protect the confidence of others covered in these records.
- Ensure that if there is any payment for the services rendered, it is fair and commensurate with the intervention provided, and within the capacity for such payment of the people served.

- Enable and encourage people to work with other individuals, organisations and groups, when such collaboration is in their best interest.
- Give consideration to all the factors in the situation, and take care to minimise possible adverse effects on the people, when the need for termination of intervention is perceived.
- Inform the people with whom they work and seek transfer or referral, with consideration to their needs and preferences, when discontinuation of intervention is anticipated.
- Do not pursue a relationship or use any coercive means to continue services, which the people served wish to terminate.

Responsibilities to society and the State

Professional social workers:

- Promote awareness and implementation of the Fundamental Rights and the Directive Principles of State Policies of the Indian Constitution, as laid down by its founders.
- Promote awareness and implementation of the United Nations Human Rights instruments, ratified by India.
- Advocate changes in social systems and the State policies, programmes and legislation to promote the values of good governance, accountability, transparency and a people-friendly approach.
- Encourage informed participation by the people in formulation of the State policies, legislation, and programmes.
- Promote professionalism in the development, implementation, monitoring and evaluation, and the dissemination of the reports of all development and welfare programmes by government departments.
- Respond and offer professional services in events of emergencies at micro- and macro-levels.

Responsibilities to co-workers and employing organisations

Professional social workers:

- Respect co-workers, which include professional and paraprofessional social workers, other professionals, volunteers and all those involved in the development process, within and across organisations.

- Contribute to working as a team, accepting and respecting personal and professional differences, through the process of collective reflection and democratic decision-making.
- Respect confidences shared by co-workers in the course of their professional relationships and transactions.
- Acknowledge co-workers' attributes and achievements and are willing to learn from them.
- Promote a practice of mutual evaluation with co-workers for each other's professional development.
- Facilitate development of the new entrants to the profession.
- Ensure clarity of goals in delegation of roles and responsibilities, provide opportunities for growth, and give due recognition to subordinates.
- Ensure that students are provided the necessary learning opportunities.
- Ensure that the organisation's resources are used judiciously and for the purpose they are intended.
- Periodically monitor and evaluate the organisation's policies and programmes, as an administrator, by using the records and feedback from people with whom they work with.

Responsibilities to social work education and research

Professional social workers:

- Are conversant with the learners' needs, readiness and goals, when teaching and training.
- Regularly update knowledge about social work profession in general and the subjects they teach, through field experience, update reading and training.
- Impart knowledge, inculcate attitudes and develop skills within the value framework of the profession, while teaching and training.
- Recognise the importance of partnership between practitioners and educators for the purpose of social work education and training.
- Develop a nurturing relationship with students, encouraging openness, critical inquiry and self study.

- Undertake people-centred field action projects as a demonstration of innovative initiatives to promote the well-being of people and for research and documentation, training and replication, whenever possible.
- Contribute to the knowledge base of social work education through practice wisdom, documentation as well as research.
- Expose the students to the professional associations and orient them about their role in developing and strengthening them.
- Carefully select the topic for research considering its possible consequences for those studied, when conducting a research.
- Do not cause the respondents any physical or mental discomfort, distress or harm, through research.
- Consider the informants of research as co-partners in understanding the phenomenon.
- Share their research objectives with them and get their informed and voluntary consent, respect their knowledge and attitude about their life situation, and share/interpret the findings with them.
- Protect the confidentiality of the information shared by them and use the findings for their benefit, by recommending and promoting policies and programmes concerning them.
- Provide information and referral services to them, as and when necessary, during the process of data collection.
- Dissociate from or do not engage in any research activity which requires manipulation, distortion or falsification of data or findings.
- Acknowledge in their written work, the published as well as unpublished material and discussions that have directly contributed to it.

Background

The 'Declaration of Ethics for Professional Social Workers', of 1997, was prepared by the Social Work Educators Forum at the Tata Institute of Social Sciences, with inputs from its faculty members, participants of a National Workshop on Social Work Practice and Education, members of the faculty of the College of Social Work at Nirmala

Niketan, members of the Bombay Association of Trained Social Workers (BATSW) and some retired social work educators. It was approved for in-house use by the Academic Council of the Tata Institute and recommended by the Association of Schools of Social Work in India for use by all the institutions for social work education in India.

In December 2000, the Committee of the UGC-sponsored Third Review of Social Work Education in India, invited feedback from all the institutions for social work education in India, on the use of and suggestions for this Declaration. Subsequently, the BATSW also sent the document to all its members for feedback. A sub-committee of the BATSW revised the document, based on the feedback received. The draft was discussed at and revised after a Maharashtra level Consultation, organised by the BATSW, on September 7, 2002.

Bombay Association of Trained Social Workers
c/o College of Social Work
Nirmala Niketan
38, New Marine Lines
Mumbai
400 020

Author Index

Subject Index

QUESTIONS OF ETHICS IN COUNSELLING AND THERAPY

Caroline Jones, (contributing ed) Carol Shillito-Clarke, Gabrielle Syme, Derek Hill, Roger Casemore and Lesley Murdin

This book offers numerous questions and answers about ethics in counselling and therapy, training, counselling supervision, research and other important issues. The authors bring psychodynamic, person-centred, integrative or eclectic approaches to their selection of questions and answers. They also bring a variety of experience from independent practice, institutional and voluntary agency settings. Between them they have experience as counsellors, psychotherapists, trainers, counselling supervisors and authors.

The questions cover a range of issues that practitioners need to consider including: confidentiality, constraints and the management of confidentiality; boundaries, dual and multiple relationships, relationships with former clients; non-discriminatory practice, issues for individuals and agencies; competence and the proper conduct of counsellors and therapists and the profession's responsibilities to deliver non-exploitative and non-abusive help to clients.

Questions of Ethics in Counselling and Therapy also contains three appendices offering useful information. It is written in a clear, accessible style and is aimed at a wide readership in counselling and therapy, ranging from trainees to more experienced practitioners.

Contents

206pp 0335 20610 7 (Paperback) 0335 20611 5 (Hardback)

RACIAL IDENTITY, WHITE COUNSELLORS AND THERAPISTS

Gill Tuckwell

This book explores the subject of racial identity and encourages readers to think freely about racial issues and to explore their own racial identity. Written from an integrative perspective, it aims to be permission-giving and to enable readers to overcome the constraints of political correctness. With a particular focus on white identity, the book challenges white therapists to develop their understanding of a relatively unexplored field. The author believes that self-awareness is an essential element of competency as a therapist, and she challenges all white therapists to be aware of what it means to be white, and how this influences the therapy process.

The book is written from a practitioner perspective, and is intended predominantly for practicing counsellors and therapists, counselling supervisors and trainers. Students and researchers in social psychology and medical sociology may also be interested in the sections on the theoretical and historical context of therapy. With an emphasis on white racial identity issues, the book is particularly relevant for white readers, however it may also enable readers from other racial groups to increase their understanding of racial development.

Contents

208pp 0335 21020 1 (Paperback) 0335 21021 X (Hardback)